Encyclopedia of Defensive Basketball Drills

Burrall Paye

Parker Publishing Company
West Nyack, New York

© 1986 by

PARKER PUBLISHING COMPANY, INC.
West Nyack, N.Y.

Library of Congress Cataloging-in-Publication Data
Paye, Burrall,
  Encyclopedia of defensive basketball drills.

  Includes index.
  1. Basketball—Defense. 2. Basketball—Coaching.
I. Title.
GV888.P385 1986   796.32'32   86-2507

ISBN 0-13-275777-X

Printed in the United States of America

How This Book Will Help You

Defensive coaches first teach their defenders the fundamentals. They then add their team defenses. Most of this defensive work is done through drills, hence the need for defensive drill books.

But most defensive drill books present isolated, nonconnecting, nonprogressive drills, leaving it to the coach to pick out the different drills he may think will help him "build" his team defense. Many times such drills produce very little improvement during practice sessions. This book can also be used in that meager manner.

But this drills book offers much much more. This book has chapters devoted entirely to man-to-man defense, to the zone defenses, to the pressure man-to-man, to half-court traps, to the full-court presses, to the drop-back traps, and to the transitional defenses. Each of these chapters have their drills presented in a connective, progressive order, designed to allow you to "build" your defense from the fundamentals up. Where drills from other chapters will also apply to help "build" another defense, proper reference is made. In this manner, a constructive "building" order can be maintained yet more space allocated so more drills can be included in the book.

Not one drill is presented just to fill space. Not one pet drill from any coach receives extensive coverage unless that drill deserves it as a progression in teaching that defense. Every drill is designed to further the development of the defense being "built."

Chapter 2, for example, presents defensive fundamental drills. Chapter 3 develops man-to-man defensive drills. But surely, you say, some drills in Chapter 2 will help to build the man-to-man defense. Yes, we reply. And everytime such a drill is offered in Chapter 2, it has a marking clearly indicating it can be used to develop the man-to-man defense. The same applies to the zone defenses (Chapter 4), the match-up zone (Chapter 5), the half-court

iii

traps (Chapter 6), the full-court man-to-man (Chapter 7), the zone presses (Chapter 8), and the fast-break defenses (Chapter 9).

And what's more—as the defenses are developed, the attackers will be improving. The book ends with a chapter filled with eighteen multipurpose drills that offer a multitude of points within each single drill. Those multiple defensive drills are appropriately marked as to the defenses they are trying to "build." This should enable you to switch drills to avoid the monotony that leads to late-season staleness.

In addition to the drills you get a whole chapter devoted to proven methods of teaching drills. In Chapter 1 you learn why it is best to present a drill in a certain way, and you will understand the make-up of the drill-teaching method completely. Even experienced coaches will find a few gems in Chapter 1.

Chapter 1 also contains a drill called the Trio Drill. It has a format like this: Drill 1: Trio Drill (3, 4, 7, 9). Each drill in the book follows the same structure: Each has a number, each has a name, and following each drill are numbers in parenthesis. These numbers in parenthesis tell the coach which team defenses these drills should be made a part of. These numbers also refer to the chapters where you find those defenses. If a letter follows the number, like 4A, it means the first defense explained in Chapter 4, namely the 2-1-2 zone defense. Also each drill number is presented on the page of defenses (the page just before Chapter 1) placing the drill with all the defenses it can help build. This gives you quick reference for collecting all the drills you need to teach your defense for the year.

Many of the drills are unique; some have been copied at regional gatherings of basketball coaches; some began in one form and were changed to fit my particular situation and philosophy. Chapter 1 will show you how to change a drill to match your situation and your philosophy.

You are the reason your practice sessions are good or bad. You cannot blame someone else. Either your method or your content prevents your practice sessions from being highly successful. This book will improve both. As your practice sessions improve, your squad gains confidence. That confidence fuels even greater confidence and better practice sessions; better practice sessions bring easier victories. Victories follow victories. And you are proud to be called *Coach.*

Burrall Paye

Content Pages of Drills

Here is the way to use this cross-reference of drills: You select the defense you intend to teach. Under that defense, all the drills that you must master to teach that chosen defense will be listed by number.

Man-to-Man

1	19	38	55	158
2	20	39	56	159
3	22	40	57	160
4	24	41	58	161
5	25	42	59	162
6	26	43	60	163
7	27	44	61	164
8	28	45	62	165
9	29	46	63	166
10	30	47	64	167
11	31	48	65	168
13	32	49	72	169
14	33	50	73	170
15	34	51	89	171
16	35	52	155	172
17	36	53	156	
18	37	54	157	

2-1-2 Zone

1	18	36	60	79
2	19	37	64	83
3	20	38	65	89
4	22	39	66	155
5	24	40	67	156
6	25	41	68	157
7	26	43	69	159
8	27	44	70	166
9	28	45	71	167
10	29	49	72	168
11	30	50	73	169
13	31	51	74	170
14	32	52	75	172
15	33	53	76	
16	34	54	77	
17	35	55	78	

1-2-2 Zone

1	19	38	66	88
2	20	39	67	89
3	22	40	68	94
4	24	41	69	95
5	25	43	70	97
6	26	44	71	104
7	27	45	72	155
8	28	49	73	156
9	29	50	74	157
10	30	51	80	159
11	31	52	81	166
13	32	53	82	167
14	33	54	83	168
15	34	55	84	169
16	35	60	85	170
17	36	64	86	172
18	37	65	87	

1-3-1 Zone

1	18	36	60	92
2	19	37	64	93
3	20	38	65	94
4	22	39	66	104
5	24	40	67	155
6	25	41	68	156
7	26	43	69	157
8	27	44	70	159
9	28	45	71	166
10	29	49	72	167
11	30	50	73	168
13	31	51	74	169
14	32	52	83	170
15	33	53	89	172
16	34	54	90	
17	35	55	91	

Match-up Zone

3	18	34	52	73	87	101
4	19	35	53	74	88	102
5	20	36	54	75	89	103
6	22	37	55	76	90	155
7	24	38	60	77	91	156
8	25	39	64	78	92	157
9	26	40	65	79	93	159
10	27	41	66	80	94	166
11	28	43	67	81	95	167
13	29	44	68	82	96	168
14	30	45	69	83	97	169
15	31	49	70	84	98	170
16	32	50	71	85	99	172
17	33	51	72	86	100	

Zone Traps

Full-Court Man-To-Man

Full-Court Zone Presses

Transition Defenses

1	16	55	117	128	146	169
3	17	94	118	129	147	170
4	21	106	119	130	148	172
6	23	107	120	131	149	
7	26	108	121	132	150	
12	27	109	124	134	151	
13	28	110	125	135	152	
14	29	111	126	140	153	
15	54	112	127	145	154	

The second part to the cross reference of drills deals with the ( ) on the drill itself. Each drill shows the following structure:

Drill 6: Quick Lateral Step Defensive Drill (3, 4, 5, 6, 7, 8, 9)

This means this drill will be used to teach man-to-man defenses (3), all different zone defenses (4), the match-up zone (5), the half-court zone traps (6), the full-court man-to-man press (7), the full-court zone presses (8), and the transitional defenses (9). The legend is

3	man-to-man defense
4A	2-1-2 zone defense
4B	1-2-2 zone defense
4C	1-3-1 zone defense
4	all zone defenses
5	match-up zone defense
6	all half-court zone traps
7	full-court man-to-man press
8	full-court zone presses
9	all types of transitional coverages

Contents

3

Man-to-Man Defensive Drills   45

4 _____

Zone Defensive Drills   69

2-1-2 Zone Defensive Drills

5

Match-Up Zone Defensive Drills   97

6

Half-Court Pressure Zone Defensive Drills   109

7 _____

Full-Court Man-to-Man Defensive Drills   117

8 _____

Full-Court Zone-Press Defensive Drills   143

9

Transition Defensive Drills 159

10

Combination of Maneuvers Defensive Drills 175

1

How to Get the Most from Your Drills

There is a vast number of drills available to the astute and resourceful basketball coach. To choose a drill that by its very design will add little or nothing to building your teams offense or defense is a foolish waste of time, and will shortly lead to your team's defeat and your early demise from the basketball-coaching fraternity. It just makes more sense to choose the drills that will build your team concepts.

To teach a correctly chosen drill haphazardly will also produce few positive results. Just as it makes sense to choose a correct drill, it also seems logical to teach it for maximum benefit. That is the two-fold purpose of this chapter: to show you how to choose the right drill, and then to explain the best mechanics to use to teach the drill.

GETTING THE RIGHT DRILL

Before you can get the right defensive drills, you have to decide on your team defenses for the year. That decision should be based on your knowledge of your returnees and your own basic defensive philosophy. Are your players quick? Are they big? At what knowledge level are they? Do you believe in man-to-man defense or zone defenses? Do you like single defenses or multiple defenses? These questions and others like them will lead you to the correct decisions.

You should begin looking for drills by late summer that will teach your contemplated defenses. You should begin by cataloging your drills. Those drills you choose should include basic fundamentals. Your selected drills should teach your defense completely. They should be progressive (from simple to complex maneuvers) and

1

detailed. Nothing should be left to chance. The drills should represent breakdowns of the various parts of your defense.

You should also choose a few drills that teach each individual phase of your defense. In that way you can alternate drills late in the season to avoid monotony that leads to staleness. The drills you introduce at the beginning of the year should teach only one small part of the fundamentals, or one minute phase of your team defense (for instance, denial of the flash pivot in man-to-man defense). As the year progresses, you would want your drills to teach two or more phases of your defense (such as contesting the vertical pass into denial of the flash pivot). If a particular area needs improvement, you can resort back to the original drill that taught that particular weakness, or you can use one of your multiple drills and make that weakness a point of emphasis. By switching back and forth from day to day, you not only improve the area under consideration but you also avoid late-season staleness.

HOW TO RECOGNIZE A GOOD DRILL

Competition. Is it competitive? If it is not, it is useless no matter how pretty it looks.

Condition. Will it condition your athletes to play your defense in game situations? If not, discard it immediately.

Simulate Game Conditions. Does it teach what actually happens in game situations? If it does not, why would you even consider it?

Forces Players to Make Decisions. Is the drill designed to have your kids programmed or does it allow for decision making by the players? You want your players to become knowledgeable about the inner workings of basketball yet stay within the framework of your team concepts. You only have four timeouts during a game, so you can't make all the decisions; you will have to teach your athletes to make some important ones.

Progressiveness. Is the drill progressive or will the drill keep your players at the same level forever? You want your players to improve by tournament time, don't you?

Time Length. You want your drills to be short in length but very productive. Most players prefer a five-minute drill to a ten-minute one. However, do not eliminate all ten-minute drills—just limit their number.

Number of Players Involved. The fewer players involved in a drill, the better the learning process. Players learn by doing. If several are constantly standing in line, they become bored and learn very little. On the other hand, if they are always actively involved, they are learning more, and faster too. They will get more repetitions of the techniques you want them to learn. Repetition of skills makes them instinctive.

By keeping the number of players in each drill to only several, your players get more repetitions. They improve much quicker. You can use managers, assistants or faculty members, to supervise groups of players at practice, thus reducing numbers required in each drill. If you can work it out so there is only one replacement player in each drill, you are on your way to a highly successful season.

Difficulty of the Drill. Use some drills that are much more difficult than game situations. Use some drills that are above the level of your players to perform well. But do not use many or you will diminish the confidence of your players.

Enjoyment. Yes, enjoyment. Players do drills they enjoy doing better than they do drudgery drills. But beware: Players too often accept drills only as something they have to do to be a member of the basketball team. Do not let this attitude creep into your drill instruction, or you will never get your players to perform at their peak level.

Relevancy. Is this drill a building stone for your defense? Do not run a drill just for the sake of drilling because somewhere you heard basketball players were supposed to be well-drilled athletes. Make sure the drill teaches a phase of your defense. Drilling just for the sake of drilling is futile, nonproductive, and time consuming. The coach who does it wastes his time, and his team derives little or no benefit from the drill.

HOW TO DRILL

Each drill must be explained in detail. Each player must understand what is to be accomplished. If you are using a drill that teaches several points but you want to improve one of the points drastically, you merely emphasize the part where you want the most improvement. You want to point out the importance of each specific maneuver a player will make as he executes the drill. You should tell the player where this particular maneuver fits into your overall team plans for the year.

You must insist that your players run the drill at full speed with enthusiasm and spirit. You may walk through a drill after

explaining it and its purpose, and make sure each player under-
stands it. Then you, as coach, must demand it be executed at full
speed. Never accept less. You can correct mistakes, but you should
not adjust the speed. Expect game speed and dismiss, not punish,
those who will not execute at game speed. Again, do not use a drill
just to drill. It will hurt the execution of the drills you use with a
purpose. Use only drills that fit perfectly into your plans for the
year. For example, if you do not intend to run a 1-2-2 zone for that
year, why would you use 1-2-2-zone defensive drills? The players
would quickly recognize such folly, and they would give less than
their maximum effort. Your next drill suffers, and the next, and the
next.

     You must never make a drill too long. At the end of each drill,
the players should want more. They are best when they want the
drill to continue, but you stop it.

     You should never, in your daily planning, place several vig-
orous drills back to back. You should try to space a less strenuous
drill between two very demanding ones. Your players may want to
give their all, but because of the spacing of your drills, they do not
have the stamina. Late in the season, when the players are at peak
condition, you might want to place two vigorous drills back to back.

     The proper formula to get the best results from a drill, re-
gardless of how many times you have run it, is threefold: Tell the
players what they are expected to get from the drill, let them run
the drill to get what was expected, and then tell the players what
they got from the drill. Each stage should receive extensive explanation. It will not be long before you have a team of intelligent
basketball players. If they are also gifted athletes, your opposition
will dread your team coming to town.

HOW TO REVISE A DRILL

     Not only do you want to develop thinking basketball players,
but you, too, have to be constantly thinking. There is never a reason
for having a bad practice. You can derive the same benefits from a
drill even if you have to alter the drill to demand that players play
harder. You, and you alone, must recognize when your team begins
to let up, and almost all players will at some point during the season. When you sense this happening, you must place responsibility
on the individual during the drill. You must especially do this while
teaching defense. Many players do not like to play defense. They
will "dog it," trying not to let you know. Every drill in this collection
can be adapted as we adapt the Trio Drill below.

Drill 1: Trio Drill (2, 3, 4, 7, 9)

Objectives:

1. To teach X1 to play one-on-one defense against a dribbler.
2. To teach X1 to block off the offensive boards, get the rebound, and throw an outlet pass.
3. To teach X1 to deny the flash pivot or contest the vertical pass; then play one-on-one defense.
4. To teach X1 the approach step, then play one-on-one defense.

Procedures:

1. Coach tosses the ball to 1. Player 1 drives on X1. Defender X1 must keep 1 under control. When 1 shoots, X1 blocks 1 off of the boards. If 1 scores, X1 throws the ball to either 2 or to 3. If 1 misses, X1 outlet passes, before he hits the floor, to either 2 or 3.
2. Let's let X1 outlet pass to 3 for explaining the drill. Actually X1 has a choice of passing to either 2 or to 3. If you plan a press for the year and 1 scores, you could require 1 to try to steal the pass into either 2 or to 3. After X1 passes to 3, 2 flash pivots. Defender X1 must deny this flash pivot. When 2 receives the pass, 2 goes one-on-one against X1. When 2 shoots, X1 rebounds and passes to 3, an outlet pass. Should 2 score, you could require 2 to try to steal the inbounds pass to 3.
3. Player X1 must approach 3 quickly but under control (the approach drill). Player 3 can, if X1 is slow to cover, score on the jump shot; 3 can also, if X1 races out too quickly, drive by X1 for the easy lay-up. If X1 gets adept at the approach drill, X1 and 3 will go one-on-one.
4. After X1 has played defense against all three, player 1 becomes the new X1, X1 becomes 2, and 2 becomes 3. Player 3 is the new 1.

This is, as you can see, an excellent individual defensive drill. It teaches several defensive points of emphasis at one time. But sooner or later, your X1 will show hard work but not really be intense on stopping 1, 2, and 3. Here is when you change the responsibilities of X1: You now tell X1 he must stop two of the three attackers or he has to go again. You must become hard-hearted. No

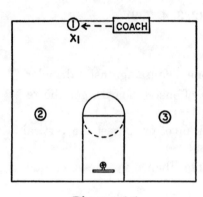

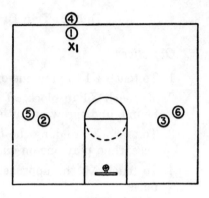

Diagram 1-1   Diagram 1-2

matter how many times X1 has to go on defense, you must keep him out there. He will either play defense or quit.

Before long, a new situation will occur. X1's teammates will not play as hard offensively so X1 will not become too depressed. Now is the time to change the attackers responsibilities. Here is what you do.

You put two offensive players in each line as shown in Diagram 1-2. To avoid having players 1, 2, and 3 not trying to score on the tired X1, you tell 1, 2, and 3 if they score they move to the end of their respective lines. So as long as 1, 2, and 3 score individually, they would never have to rotate to play defense. They will never have to become an X1. For example, 1 scores and goes to the end of his line. This moves 4 up front. 2 and 3 do not score. So the rotation begins: X1 to the end of 2's line, 2 to the end of 3's line, and 3 behind 1 in the first line. 1 now attacks 4, who is the new X1. If 1 scores, he moves behind 3. As long as 1 scores, he will never have to rotate to defense. The same is true for players 2 and 3 initially. This method encourages each offensive player to do as well as he can, for each player must fear, should they become the defender, they may have to play defense three, four, five, or more times. Before long, the weaker defenders improve, your team defense improves, and your attackers and defenders play with the intensity and concentration you see in champions.

All the drills in this book can be worked in the same competitive manner. Your requirements determine how good your practice sessions will be, and your practice sessions determine the level your ball club will rise to.

2

Defensive Fundamental Drills

Before any team defense can be developed to its maximum potential, individual defenders must become proficient at not only handling the attacker they are guarding (man defense) or the area they are responsible for (zone defense), but also at defending an unlimited number of recurrent offensive situations. Some of those repeated elements include stopping an open attacker who is driving for a basket, forcing a hurried jump shot, denying the pass to an inside cutter, and defending the stationary post. These components will appear and reappear whether your team is playing man-to-man defense, or a zone, or a combination. They are called the fundamentals of defensive basketball.

By drilling your players again and again and again on these fundamentals, you make their coverage instinctive. When this coverage becomes involuntary, your defenders will always enjoy a step advantage, both mentally and physically, on their attackers. So your first building block is to drill, drill, and further drill the pertinent sections of this chapter: those are, those drills relevant to your chosen team defense.

Drill 2: Held-Ball Drill (3, 4, 6)

Objectives:

1. To teach attackers to protect the ball by pivoting properly.
2. To teach the offensive step-through move to avoid double-team pressure.
3. To teach defenders the proper techniques of gaining a held ball without fouling.

Procedure:

1. Line up your team with one attacker and two defenders in each group (Diagram 2–1).
2. Give the attacker a ball. The attacker has lost his dribble. The attacker must learn to pivot, keeping the ball away from the two defenders.
3. The two defenders try to get one or two hands on the ball, trying to force a held-ball situation without fouling or trying to pry the ball out of the attacker's hands.
4. Let each attacker have the ball for 30 seconds. Total time of the drill: one and one-half minutes.
5. After an attacker steps through for thirty seconds, one of the two defenders becomes the next attacker. The player who began as an attacker becomes a defender.

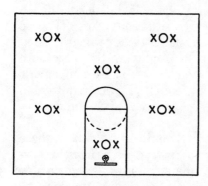

Diagram 2-1

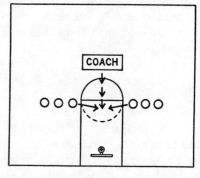

Diagram No. 2-2

Drill 3: Quick Hands Individual Drill (3, 4, 5, 6, 7, 8, 9)

Objectives:

1. To teach quick aggressive hands.
2. To teach player how to slap at a loose ball for recovery.
3. To teach recovery of loose balls.
4. To teach one-on-one defensive and offensive techniques.
5. To teach instant conversion from offensive play to defensive play.
6. To teach hustling defense.

Procedure:

1. Two lines should be formed near a line on the court (Diagram 2-2).
2. Have first two players step out to the middle of the free throw or centercourt line.
3. Coach can require players to place hands on knees, hands in proper defensive position, hands immediately in front of face, or anywhere the coach wants the defender's hands.
4. Coach tosses ball waist high between the defenders, or he can bounce the ball off of the floor waist high. Two players try to recover the loose ball. Player recovering loose ball is on offense; the other player is on defense. They play a one-on-one game. After a score the players go to the end of the opposite line.
5. The next two players step to the center of the free throw or centercourt line and the drill continues.

Drill 4: Quick Foot Movement (3, 4, 5, 6, 7, 8, 9)

Objectives:

1. To teach defensive foot quickness.
2. To condition players to play in a crouched position for long periods of time.

Procedure:

1. Three players place their feet on A and B: right foot on A, left foot on B (Diagram 2–3).
2. Several different quickness drills begin from the above foot positions:
   a. Players jump in with right foot touching C; then out with right foot hitting D and left foot hitting F. The player immediately makes a 180 degree turn putting his left foot on D and his right foot on F. Player puts right foot on C; then he jumps out with left foot hitting on A and right foot on B. Then the player executes another 180 degree turn. This process continues.
   b. Instead of originally jumping into C with right foot, player could begin with left foot; and the same process continues.

    c. Instead of originally jumping into C with right foot, player could jump into C with both feet.

    d. You could begin with player's left foot on A and right foot on B. The player's back is to the coach. The player jumps into the C block backward landing with both feet, with the right foot, or with the left foot (whichever you wish). Then the player jumps out with left foot on D and right foot on F. A 180 degree turn would then have the athlete facing the coach. The process then continues.

3. You want to allow 25 seconds and record the number of full revolutions each athlete manages. As they get quicker, the number will increase immeasurably.

4. Because quickness is the important test on defense, athletes do not want to raise their feet off of the floor. Neither do they want to drag their feet along the floor—the friction between the shoe and floor would reduce quickness. Neither do you want the athlete to hop. You want him to glide quickly, lifting his feet ever so slightly. The athlete wants to have the sensation of his toes grabbing at the floor as he slides through the drill.

5. This drill is an excellent psychological defensive drill. It makes the athlete think quickness, an attribute seen in all great defenders.

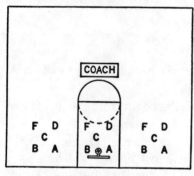

Diagram 2-3

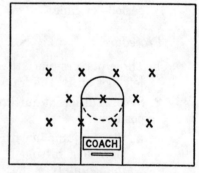

Diagram 2-4

Drill 5: The All-Important First-Step Drill (3, 4, 5)

Objectives:

1. To teach stance.

2. To teach first-step movement, the most important step in both offense and defense.

3. To teach concentration and anticipation, prerequisites to quickness.

Procedure:

1. You can use only one defender with a coach facing him, preferably at a line on the court; or you can begin the drill as a mass drill (Diagram 2-4).
2. The player moves only one step in the direction the coach moves. Coach should establish a pivot foot, and he should use a basketball.
3. The defender should take a long step. He wants to work on the advance step, the retreat step, and the swing step.
4. The player should be in a perfect defensive stance, and he must react quickly.
5. The coach must constantly check the stance and perfect it.
6. The coach steps forward, the defender retreats with the foot where the coach stepped (the retreat step). The coach brings his foot back to beginning position; the defender recovers to his beginning position (the advance step). The coach uses a cross-over step; the defender answers with a swing step.

Drill 6: Quick Lateral-Step Defensive Drill (3, 4, 5, 6, 7, 8, 9)

Objectives:

1. To teach quick lateral foot movement needed for defense.
2. To develop defensive conditioning.

Procedure:

1. Line up four or five players in the lane with a coach facing the players (Diagram 2-5).
2. Players must get down in a defensive stance as though they are guarding an attacker who intends to drive to the basket. On dribbles, we advocate the parallel stance. Your defenders should be able to touch the floor with the palms of their hands as they slide. This keeps them in a low defensive position.
3. Coach begins his timing with 60 seconds, intending to advance to 90 seconds.
4. Player must place their lead foot outside the lane as they slide from side to side.

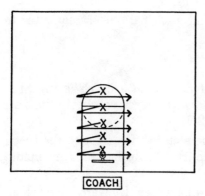
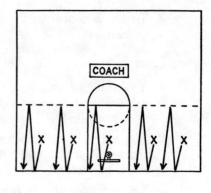

Diagram 2-5   Diagram 2-6

5. Coach should record the number of completed revolutions by each player. This should improve with each workout.

6. While defenders slide, they should not let their feet drag along the floor. Neither should they hop. Foot quickness is the important development.

Drill 7: Quick Vertical-Step Defensive Drill (3, 4, 5, 6, 7, 8, 9)

Objectives:

1. To teach vertical defensive sliding quickness.
2. To develop defensive conditioning.

Procedure:

1. Line up four or five players facing the coach (Diagram 2-6).
2. Coach times the slides. Start with 60 seconds and work up to 90 seconds.
3. Record the number of complete revolutions by each player.
4. You could have your players run their slides in several different ways:

   a. *Backward:* You can have the players slide sideways as they retreat, simulating stopping a driving attacker; or you can have players slide backward as though they are trying to intercept a pass lobbed downcourt.

   b. *Forward:* You can have players race forward hard, trying to arrive to an attacker as the ball arrives; or you can have the players slide forward, using the approach step.

5. Be sure players slide without hopping and without allowing shoe-floor friction.

6. You can extend the boundaries from baseline to top of the circle or to the 28-foot marker or to midcourt. Whatever distance you choose, you want to put tape down or draw a line with chalk. You want to require the athletes' lead foot to touch the line or go over it.

Drill 8: Mass-Denial Sliding Drill (3, 6, 7, 8)

Objectives:

1. To condition legs in normal guarding (denial) position.
2. To teach defensive movement that must be used to deny inbounds passes, vertical passes, and passes into the middle.
3. To teach visual reaction and concentration.
4. To develop quickness of the feet.

Procedure:

1. Players are to get down in normal fencing position as shown in Diagram 2-7. Feet are to be at right angles, hands out front as if the defenders are holding a foil.
2. Players are to use fence slides as though they are attacking.
3. On visual command, the coach has the players advance, retreat, advance, retreat, until they go the full length of the court.
4. Coach must be careful that players keep their body balanced (weight evenly distributed) and that their feet do not slide along the floor, creating friction that slows the defender. Defensive players should never let the knee of their front foot advance over the toe of that foot. Start the drill slowly being sure that the proper balance is always kept.

Drill 9: Combination Slide Drill (3, 4, 5, 6)

Objectives:

1. To teach defenders to recognize which slide to use and to use it quickly.
2. To condition defensively.

Procedure:

1. Line up three or four players facing a coach (Diagram 2-8).
2. Coach has a basketball and establishes a pivot foot.

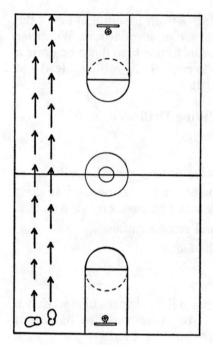

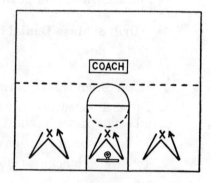

Diagram 2-8

Diagram 2-7

3. Coach steps forward, backward, or dribbles a dribble sideways. Players react with an advance step, a retreat step, or a lateral step.

4. Coach can require a player to immediately slide back to his original starting position, or the coach can continue his dribble and steps without having player return to starting position.

5. Coach can cross over, requiring defenders to use swing step. Coach can turn his back to the defender (reverse dribble), requiring players to drop step preparing for their defense of the reverse dribble.

Drill 10: Triangle Defensive Stance Drill (3, 4, 5)

Objectives:

1. To teach the lateral slide.
2. To teach the swing step.
3. To teach the approach step.
4. To teach the retreat step.
5. To condition the legs for all-out defensive play.

Procedure:

1. Line up players as shown in Diagram 2-9.
2. Players slide for as long as you, the coach, desires.
3. You should do the completed triangle at least twice, then reverse the directions.
4. Three players can be going on the triangle at one time. Start the second player when the first turns the corner.

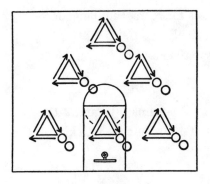

Diagram 2-9

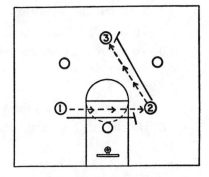

Diagram 2-10

Drill 11: Defensive Circle Drill (3, 4, 5)

Objectives:

1. To teach defenders the approach step, the advance step, the retreat step, and the swing step.
2. To teach defenders the front-foot-to-pivot-foot stance.
3. To teach attackers the crossover, the jab-step, the rocker steps, and the reverse-pivot fakes.

Procedure:

1. Line players up as shown in Diagram 2-10.
2. Player 1 passes to 2. Player 1 goes to defend 2; 2 chooses a pivot foot as 1 is on his way. Player 2 can jab step, crossover step, jab step then crossover, pivot into a reverse move, etc.
3. The steps by 2 require that 1 use the retreat step, the advance step, and the swing step. Player 1 also has to use the approach step when he approaches 2; 1 must make intelligent choices.
4. After 2 has tried the steps described above, 2 passes to 3.

Player 2 goes to defend 3; 3 then chooses a pivot foot and the drill continues.

5. Player 1 stays at 2's location. When 3 passes, 3 goes to defend whomever he passes to. Player 2 will stay at 3's location.

Drill 12: Sliding Drill—Half Court (6, 7, 8, 9)

Objectives:

1. To teach the backward slides for retreating defenders.
2. To condition the legs defensively.
3. To improve defensive body balance.

Procedure:

1. Line up players as shown in Diagrams 2-11 and 2-12.
2. Do the drill at both ends of the court as quickly as the

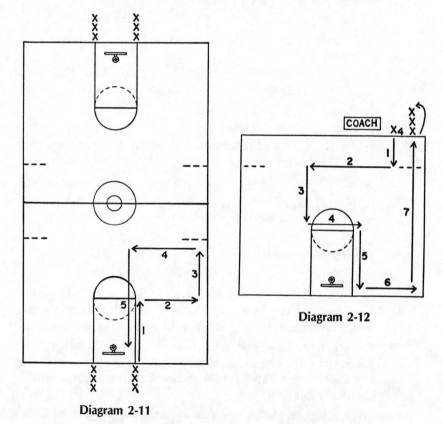

Diagram 2-12

Diagram 2-11

defenders can correctly do them. You can do the drill several times before going to another drill.

3. In both diagrams, slide 1 is backward, slide 2 is a parallel slide, slide 3 is backward, slide 4 is a parallel slide, and slide 5 is a backward slide. Slides 6 and 7 are only in Diagram 2-12: Slide 6 is a parallel slide and slide 7 is an all-out sprint forward.

4. You can add talking on the second trip through the drill, and you can require sliding with the palms of the hands touching the floor on the third trip.

5. You can have the players race hard backward on the backward slides, or you can have the players race sideways as though they are looking to intercept a long lob pass.

Drill 13: Sliding the Line Palms Down Drill (3, 4, 5, 6, 7, 8, 9)

Objectives:

1. To teach players to slide quickly without coming out of their defensive stance.
2. To condition legs for long periods of defensive play and for full-court defensive pressure.

Procedure:

1. Line up all players at the endline (Diagram 2-13).
2. Players first slide to their left as though in a parallel stance covering a nonpenetrating dribbler.
3. Players then slide backward up the sideline to half court.
4. Players slide to their right using a parallel slide.
5. Players slide backward down the sideline (right).
6. Players slide left using a parallel slide along the near baseline.
7. Players slide forward up to midcourt using the approach step.
8. Players slide right using the parallel stance.
9. Players slide forward back to their beginning position using the approach step.
10. Begin by going once around the floor and work up to going four times around the floor without stopping. Between every slide, players are to put their palms on the floor without bobbing. You could use the same route but require different slides.

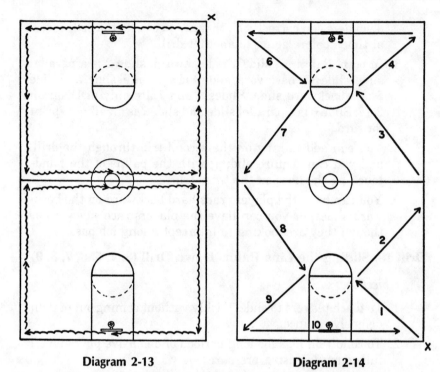

Diagram 2-13   Diagram 2-14

 Drill 14: Sliding Drill—Full Court (3, 4, 5, 6, 7, 8, 9)

Objectives:

1. To teach the steps (retreat, advance, and swing) used in playing defensive basketball.
2. To condition the legs so the defenders can stay in a low defensive stance for an entire game.
3. To teach defensive communication.
4. To teach sliding backward, laterally, and forward, using whichever technique the coach desires.

Procedure:

1. Line up players as shown in Diagram 2-14.
2. You can go through the slides one, two, or three times.
3. Slide 1: retreat slide to the defender's right—swing step at the free throw line. Slide 2: retreat slide to defender's left with a swing step at midcourt line. Slide 3: retreat slide to the defender's right and a swing step at the free throw line.

Slide 4: a left retreat slide with a swing step at the baseline. Slide 5: a parallel slide to the right. This drill continues with the defender always facing the baseline he began on. This should give the defender drills on all defensive slides.

4. Once through emphasizing the sliding step only. Then have the defender talk, not just talking but using terms used in your proposed defensive structure. Then have the defender slide touching the floor with the palms of his hands as he slides.

Drill 15: Full-Court Talking Drill (3, 4, 5, 6, 7, 8, 9)

Objectives:

1. To teach defensive communication.
2. To teach defensive sliding, staying low without bobbing heads.
3. To condition legs for pressing an entire game.

Procedure:

1. Line up all players on end line as shown in Diagram 2-15.
2. First player in line races backward to the 28-foot line where he pivots facing out-of-bounds. He defensively slides to the free throw line extended (left sideline), hitting the palms of his hands on the floor with each slide. He again slides facing midcourt after his pivot. He slides defensively to the opposite sideline (right), then races backward to the point where the left sideline intersects the midcourt line. He slides across the midcourt line telling his teammates what he sees in front of him, helping them avoid pileups. When he reaches the right sideline at midcourt, he races backward to the free throw line extended on the left sideline. He pivots, facing the end line, and slides defensively to the right sideline. When he touches the right sideline, he pivots, looking inward, and slides up to the 28-foot marker. From there, he races backward to the end line. While racing through this maze, he constantly crosses the paths of his teammates. Both he and his teammates have their backs to each other. Only through talking will they circumvent contact. Defensive players should touch the palms of their hands on the floor with every defensive slide. They should accomplish this without bobbing their heads.

3. Second player in the line begins racing backward when the first player reaches the first free throw line.

4. A trip downcourt and back by each player takes less than a minute. You can require one or more trips, depending on the communication skills of the defenders.

5. You can alter what is said by having spots where defensive calls must be made. Calls should include terminology used in your team defense: "switch," "jump," "trap," "rotate," and so on. You choose the language and the spots on the floor where you want a particular term used.

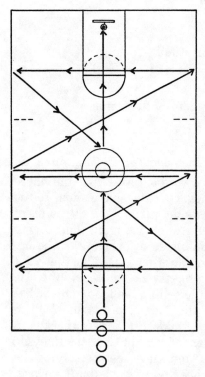

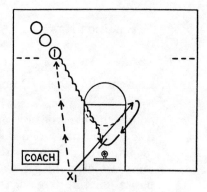

Diagram 2-16

Diagram 2-15

Drill 16: Drawing-the-Charge Drill (3, 4, 5, 6, 7, 8, 9)

Objectives:

1. To teach drawing the charge under game conditions.

2. To teach hustling defense and recognizing when to draw the charge.

3. To teach an attacker to drive hard to the basket, not worrying about the contact of charging.

Procedure

1. Line up players as shown in Diagram 2-16.
2. Rotate from offense to defense to the end of the line. First man in line becomes the next 1.
3. X1 rolls the ball to 1. Player 1 races hard to get the ball; then 1 begins to dribble, driving hard to the basket. Meanwhile, X1 has touched the opposite free throw line, and X1 must hurry back to get proper defensive position to draw the charge.
4. Coach calls whether it is a charge or a block.
5. You can alter the drill by requiring that 1 dive for the loose ball before getting up and driving hard to the basket. When using this phase of the drill, you should shorten 1's distance or lengthen X1's.

Drill 17: Mass Drawing-the-Charge Drill (3, 4, 5, 6, 7, 8, 9)

Objective:

1. To teach defenders how to draw the charge without getting hurt.

Procedure:

1. Line up the entire squad about fifteen feet apart as shown in Diagram 2-17.
2. On the whistle, the attackers begin driving hard straight across the court.
3. On the same whistle, the defenders take a step or two toward the driver and prepare for the contact. On contact, the defenders push off the balls of their feet and land on their buttocks. The defenders roll over to their sides after landing, raising their top leg. This should prevent injury except for the minor bruises and aches that come with contact and with falling on the floor.

Drill 18: One-on-One under Control (3, 4, 5)

Objectives:

1. To teach your defensive stance on the ball handler (ours is front foot to pivot foot).

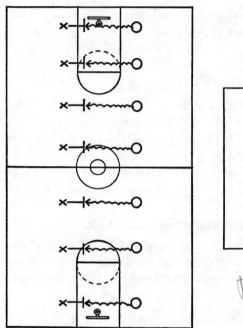

Diagram 2-17

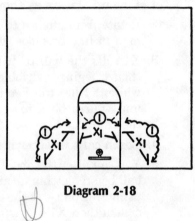

Diagram 2-18

2. To teach defenders to cover a dribbler who may drive or shoot.

3. To teach good defense of the jump shot. Defender moves to cover his man when both hands of the dribbler touch the ball.

4. Your players can learn new offensive moves, and they learn to shoot under pressure.

5. To teach defense of the pump fakes.

Procedure:

1. Player 1 begins with a basketball and may use any fake he desires (Diagram 2–18).

2. When first teaching the drill, don't let 1 dribble. Then, advance him to one dribble, then two dribbles. Begin by letting 1 attack in only one direction. Then allow him both directions.

3. Player 1 may shoot when he gets X1 off balance but never allow a forced shot.

4. Player X1 begins in front-foot-to-pivot-foot stance (use your defensive stance on the ball).

5. Player X1 must not leave his feet until 1 has left his.

6. Player X1 must keep his hand extended, making his reach four inches longer.

7. Coach can stand where X1 does not see him, hold up fingers to allow 1 that many dribbles. We limit it at first to dribbles in only one direction. We start out with no dribble, then move to one, then two.

8. You can require 1 to use his right foot as a pivot foot one time, then the left foot as the pivot foot the next time.

9. You can move 1 under the basket and let him use his pump fakes. Player X1 must not allow 1 an uncontested shot. Player X1 leaves his feet as 1 leaves his. Player X1 extends himself, not trying to block the shot, but trying to force 1 to raise his shot.

Drill 19: Just One-on-One (3, 4, 5)

Objectives:

1. To teach X1 and X3 how to control the driver, yet pressure the jump shot.

2. To teach 1 and 3 offensive moves from their positions.

3. To teach offensive and defensive rebounding.

Procedure:

1. Line up players as shown in Diagram 2-19.

2. Rotate from offense to defense to end of opposite line. First player in each line becomes the new offensive player.

3. Begin the drill by limiting the area 1 and 3 may use to score. Also, limit the number of dribbles the attackers may use.

4. Begin by alternating one-on-one plays by each line. After a few days let both lines go at the same time. This forces the defensive men to feel for any possible interference from the other line.

5. Begin by not letting the defense use their hands.

6. After X1 and X3 start controlling 1 and 3, let 1 and 3 have the entire court to operate, and let X1 and X3 have the use of their hands.

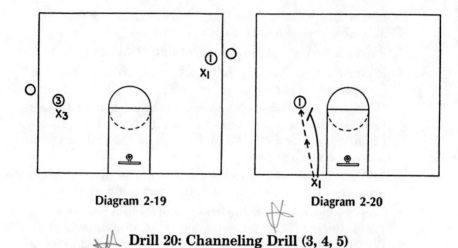

Diagram 2-19   Diagram 2-20

Drill 20: Channeling Drill (3, 4, 5)

Objectives:

1. To teach defenders the slowness of the bounce pass.
2. To teach X1 the approach step: to get to 1 without giving 1 the advantage.
3. To teach X1 to think defensively.
4. To teach X1 to channel 1 where X1 wants to go, teaching controlling and dominating the offense.
5. To teach X1 to instantly recognize which foot is 1's pivot foot.
6. To teach X1 to force his offensive man to cut toward his pivot foot (our defensive idea—you choose where you want 1 to cut). That is the offensive man's most awkward and slowest direction.

Procedure:

1. X1 passes to 1, then races to defend against him (Diagram 2–20).
2. X1 should use the bounce pass: it is slower. Player 1 cannot leave until he receives the pass. Player 1 chooses a pivot foot; X1 must recognize that pivot foot.
3. You could require X1 to alter his channeling route: one time cut 1 inside, the next time cut 1 outside. To do this we have to have 1 switch his pivot foot because of our front-foot-to-pivot-foot stance.

Drill 21: Cut Inside or Outside Drill (7, 8, 9)

Objectives:

1. To teach stopping a driver on a fast break or after having broken a press.
2. To teach visual concentration.
3. To teach the defense how to prevent a driver from turning the corner.
4. To teach cutting inside or outside (your choice).
5. To teach full-speed ball handing.
6. To teach defense to stay in motion—use parallel stance until the defense decides which way to cut the offense, then slide with the trail foot as the advance foot in a staggered stance.
7. To teach defenders how to delay an offensive man who is advancing the ball on a fast break (this is used after the attackers are allowed to change directions).

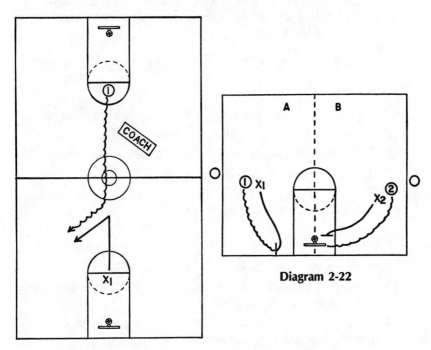

Diagram 2-21

Diagram 2-22

Procedure:

1. An offensive man begins at his defensive foul line and dribbles at full speed toward the opposite basket (Diagram 2–21).
2. When the offense reaches half court, the coach, who is standing behind the dribbler, signals the defense which way to cut the offense.
3. The defender is in motion, using the pat-the-floor motion.
4. The defender must cut the offensive man in the direction the coach has signaled.
5. The defender is to cut the offensive man out-of-bounds before he can turn the corner. The defender can do this by staying one-quarter a man's length behind the dribbler, using quick shuffle steps. The defender must also use the proper cushion so that he will not get beaten. The proper cushion varies directly with the speed of the two men involved.
6. At first the offensive man is not allowed to reverse his direction; but, when the defense becomes proficient, we permit change of directions.

Drill 22: Covering the Baseline-Corner Driver (3, 4, 5)

Objectives:

1. To teach the two methods of covering the baseline drive.
2. To teach the proper angle to cut off the offensive man.
3. To teach offensive men to drive the baseline correctly.
4. To teach drawing the charge.
5. To teach offensive men to jump back into the court without charging and still score.

Procedure:

1. Line up players as shown in Diagram 2-22.
2. Put a line on each side of the court—rotate from offense to defense to the end of the other line.
3. Player X1 cuts 1 baseline, then races and cuts off 1 by placing his left foot on the baseline.
4. Player X2 allows 2 to drive the baseline, then tries to draw the charge as 2 jumps back into X2 on his scoring attempt;

X2 must keep his shoulders parallel to and directly underneath the backboard. Player X2's arms must be held straight up toward the ceiling, eliminating any doubt in the official's mind.

5. Switch the side of the court from day to day for drills A and B.

Drill 23: Full-Court Zigzag Drill (6, 7, 8, 9)

Objectives:

1. To teach cutoffs by defensive overplays.
2. To teach pressure defense over the full-court.
3. To condition defensively.
4. To teach advancing the ball offensively under extreme pressure.
5. To teach offense and defense of the reverse and crossover dribbles.

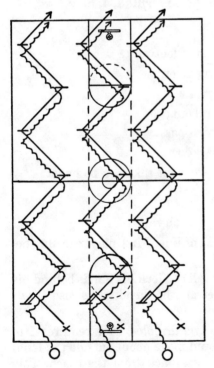

Diagram 2-23

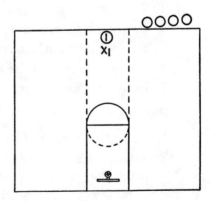

Diagram 2-24

Procedure:

1. Divide teams into pairs: one offense, one defense. Put your point guards and best defenders in the middle lane (Diagram 2–23).
2. The offense advances the ball.
3. The defense is to race back and turn the offense by use of an overplay.
4. We start the season without the use of hands, progressing to handwork after footwork is mastered.
5. Defenders must turn attacker at least three times in each half court.
6. We let offense go down and back; then we switch from offense to defense.
7. You can, in the early stages, require that the offense use only the reverse or only the crossover. You can then advance to allowing them the use of both.

Drill 24: One-on-One Lane Drill (3, 4, 5)

Objectives:

1. To teach one-on-one defensive footwork.
2. To teach defense of the crossover.
3. To teach defense of the reverse.
4. To teach blocking out on rebounds.
5. To teach denial of the return pass.
6. To teach defense of the backdoor.
7. To teach offense to attack without taking a bad shot.

Procedure:

1. Line up players as shown in Diagram 2-24.
2. Rotate from 1 to X1 to end of line. First player in line becomes the next 1.
3. Begin the drill by requiring X1 to lock his hands behind his back. He must use his feet and his head; otherwise 1 will score all night.
4. You can limit player 1 to two dribbles. This requires 1 to pass to the coach (who should move about outside the lane) and to get open to get a pass back from the coach. This means X1 will have plenty of opportunities to deny the pass back to 1, thereby perfecting his denial defense.

5. You can limit 1 to crossover moves only. You can limit him to reverses. You can give him both. To stop the crossover, X1 should slide in the direction of the dribble but use his trail hand to swipe at the ball. To stop the reverse X1 would drop his foot in the direction of the reverse and recover to try to draw the charge.
6. Once 1 passes to the coach, X1 should contest the pass back to 1.
7. Player 1 can never get out of the lane—he must attack within the dotted lines.
8. Player X1 must box out when 1 shoots. Only 1 can rebound. Player X1 must let the carom hit the floor. When missed shots hit the floor, the drill is over and everyone rotates. You must make X1 stay on defense until he stops 1. Don't feel sorry for X1, or X1 will never be the defender you want him to be.

Drill 25: Defending the Individual Drive Moves (3, 4, 5)

Objectives:

1. To teach attackers the dribble reverse, crossover, and other moves.
2. To teach defensive footwork against the dribbling reverse and the dribbling crossover.
3. To teach defense of the reverse, the defender must get a half step in front of the driver. If the driver continues, the defender draws the charge. When the defender sees the attacker square up sideways, the defender quickly races to the opposite side, anticipating the reverse.
4. To teach drawing the charge.
5. To teach defensive overplays.

Procedure:

1. Player 1 can use the dribbling reverse only (later add the crossover). He may use any other fake he would like, such as change of pace, head and shoulder fakes, etc. to try to free himself but he must reverse (later crossover) when he changes directions. After defensing the reverse, work on defensing the crossover. Then give the attacker the right to use either or both (Diagram 2–25).
2. To defend against the crossover, the trail hand should swipe at the dribble as the defender slides in the direction of the

dribbler. This coverage could result in forcing a turnover; it also prevents the dribbler from gaining an advantage should the defender not deflect the ball.

3. Player 1 can change direction whenever he wishes, but he cannot go outside the free throw line and he must use the crossover or the reverse, whichever is designated.

4. Player X1 must constantly hustle back into an overplay, causing 1 to reverse or crossover to change his direction.

5. Start the drill in the early season without letting X1 use his hands; progress to hand action in about one week (longer if defenders do not gain proficiency in foot movement).

6. Encourage X1 to draw the charge, using defensive hand fakes (when given hands), and head and shoulder fakes.

7. After mastering the defensive techniques, give the offense more area in which to operate, such as the entire left side of the half court.

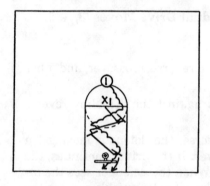

Diagram 2-25

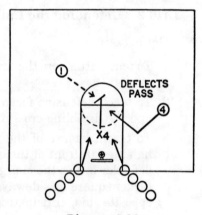

Diagram 2-26

Drill 26: Deny, Deflect, and Recover (3, 4, 5, 9)

Objectives:

1. To teach defense of the flash pivot.

2. To teach defensive hustle and alertness.

3. To teach recovery of loose balls.

4. To teach one-on-one play offensively and defensively.

5. To teach instant conversion from offense to defense.

6. To teach the offensive dip, change of pace, and change of direction.

Procedure:

1. Line players up as shown in Diagram 2-26.

2. Rotate from 1 to 4 to X4 to end of the left line to the end of the right line. First player in right line becomes the new 1.

3. Player 4 dips and breaks into the flash pivot; X4 cuts him off, beating him to the most favored spot, and deflects the pass.

4. The two lines race for the deflected ball. They cannot leave until the defender (X4) touches the ball. The player who comes up with the loose ball is on offense; the other one is on defense in a one-on-one half-court game. You can designate the basket at the other end of the court as the area where the one-on-one game is to take place. This forces full-court decisions by your defenders.

Drill 27: Straight-Line Tough-Fight One-on-One (3, 4, 5, 9)

Objectives:

1. To teach aggressive hustle to recover a loose ball.

2. To teach individual defense and individual offense.

3. To develop a competitive atmosphere among your defenders.

Procedure:

1. Line up players as shown in Diagram 2-27.

2. Coach rolls ball down the middle of the floor. He should vary the speed and the distance.

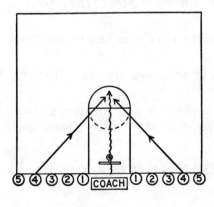

Diagram 2-27

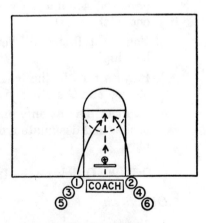

Diagram 2-28

3. Coach calls a number and those two race out to get the ball,
   diving if necessary to recover it.
4. The player who recovers the ball becomes the attacker and
   the other becomes the defender. They play one-on-one back
   to the basket, and then they return to their spot in the line.
5. Coach can make the drill highly competitive and keep score
   to a total number of baskets. He can put guards on one team
   and big men on the other, seniors on one team and under-
   classmen on the other, or starters on one team and sub-
   stitutes on the other.
6. Coach can make it a full-court transition drill by designat-
   ing the basket at the opposite end of the court as the one-on-
   one basket after the recovery has been made.

Drill 28: Aggressiveness and One-on-One (3, 4, 5, 9)

Objectives:

1. To teach aggressiveness.
2. To teach one-on-one offense and defense.
3. To teach players to dive on the floor for loose balls.
4. To teach instant conversion from offense to defense.
5. To teach cutting an attacker in one direction.

Procedure:

1. Line players up in two lines (Diagram 2-28). Diagram 2-28
   exhibits the lines at the intersection of the free throw and
   baselines. You can line up in the two corners or at midcourt
   or on the side lines. You can put the players at the opposite
   end of the court.
2. You can roll the ball down the middle, or can bounce the
   ball high.
3. Players race to the ball. Player recovering the ball is on
   offense and the other is on defense.
4. You can play at only one basket. Or you can start at one
   basket and designate a different basket for the one-on-one
   play.

Drill 29: Quick Feet—Individual Drill (3, 4, 5, 9)

Objectives:

1. To teach the defensive lateral slide.
2. To teach hustling defense.

3. To teach instant conversion from offense to defense.

4. To teach one-on-one offensive and defensive techniques.

5. To teach recovery of loose balls.

Procedure:

1. Line up players as shown in Diagram 2-29.

2. Roll the ball slowly up the floor. On signal, X1 and X2 slide to the corner around the ball and race to recover the loose ball.

3. Player who recovers the ball is on offense. The other player is on defense. They play one-on-one.

4. After those two play one-on-one, they go to the end of the line. The first two players in the line prepare to chase down the next loose ball.

5. You can have players play one-on-one at the beginning basket, or you can designate another basket for the one-on-one play.

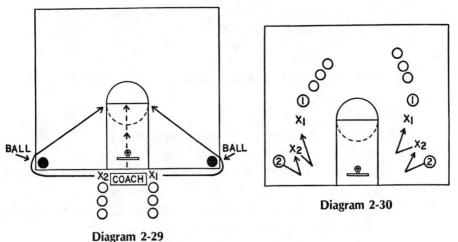

Diagram 2-29

Diagram 2-30

Drill 30: Forward Denial (3, 4, 5)

Objectives:

1. To drill on the fence slide by X2. He must keep 2 from receiving a pass below the free throw line extended.

2. To teach 2 the offensive dip to free himself for a pass or to teach 2 to reverse pivot and square-out to receive a pass.

3. To teach 1 to pass under pressure.

4. To teach X1 the step-in-and-toward-every-pass principle.

5. To teach one-on-one defense including the stances.

6. To teach one-on-one offense.

7. To teach X1 to zone it (a basic man-to-man as well as zone principle).

8. To teach X1 to close the gap on inside drives.

Procedure:

1. Line up players as shown in Diagram 2-30.

2. Rotation would be from 1 to X1, X1 to 2, 2 to X2, X2 to the end of the line. New 1 comes from front of the line.

3. Player 2 takes a deep dip and X2 fence slides, trying to prevent 2 from receiving a pass from 1.

4. Player 1 must throw pass to 2 on the side away from the defense. Once 1 has completed the pass, X1 jumps one and a half steps toward 2 and one step in to the basket.

5. After 2 has received the pass, he goes one-on-one against X2 until 2 is stopped or scores.

6. Player X2 must be able to cover the baseline. He will have help, X1, on all inside drives. We start by not letting 1 move, then progress by giving 1 free reign in movement.

Drill 31: Deny Ball Reversal and Defend (3, 4, 5)

Objectives:

1. To teach X1 to play one-on-one defense without allowing dribbling penetration.

2. To teach X1 to deny passes back around the top of the key.

3. To teach X1 to defense the backdoor cuts of 1.

4. To teach 1 to receive a pass and go immediately into an attacking triple-threat position.

5. To teach defensive and offensive rebounding.

6. To teach 1 not to take a bad shot.

Procedure:

1. Line players up as shown in Diagram 2-31.

2. Rotate from 1 to X1 to 2 to 3 to end of line. First player in line becomes the new 1.

3. Player 1 starts near midcourt and can only dribble inside the lane lines extended. We begin by giving 1 only two

dribbles and we may extend the number of dribbles to an unlimited number when X1 has mastered controlling the dribbler.

4. In the beginning stages 1 can only shoot a lay-up. As the season progresses, we allow the jump shot.

5. If 1 cannot score, he must not take a bad shot; instead he passes to 2 or to 3. Then X1 jumps toward the pass and tries to deny a pass back to 1. This procedure continues until X1 steals the ball or 1 scores.

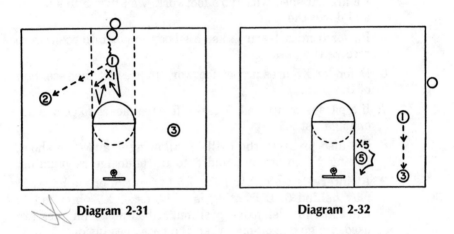

Diagram 2-31   Diagram 2-32

Drill 32: Defensing the Side and Low Post (3, 4, 5)

Objectives:

1. To teach proper defensive footwork by side-pivot and low-post defenders.

2. To teach offensive and defensive one-on-one play from the side and the low-post positions.

3. To teach rebounding offensively and defensively.

4. To teach fronting, playing behind, and playing three-quarter side positions.

5. To teach proper perimeter passing in order to get the ball inside.

6. To teach correct methods of passing into the pivot.

7. To teach 5 to post up properly: proper use of hand signals and use of the body are required to receive the pass.

8. To teach offensive moves, such as the drop step, upon receiving the pass inside.

Procedure:

1. Line up players on side of the court as shown in Diagram 2-32.
2. Rotate from 1 to 3 to X5 to 5 to end of the line. First man in line takes the 1 position.
3. Players 1 and 3 drill on their passing techniques until they can pass to 5. No lob passes are permitted.
4. Player 5 must stand still at the beginning of the drill. After we are satisfied with X5's footwork, we allow 5 to slide up and down the lane.
5. Player 5 must learn to use his body to get into position to receive the pass.
6. Defender X5 uses proper footwork to prevent the reception of the pass.
7. If a pass is completed, 5 uses offensive moves to go one-on-one against X5.
8. We also progress the drill by allowing 1 and 3 to shoot, forcing X5 to box out and 5 to try offensive rebounding.
9. At intervals we either have X5 to front 5, or we have X5 play behind 5. If fronting is to be used, X5 plays tag to maintain his defensive position; if behind techniques are used, we go one-on-one when the pass goes inside.

Drill 33: Deny the Flash Pivot (3, 4, 5, 6, 7, 8)

Objectives:

1. To teach X3 proper methods and techniques of defensing a flash pivot.
2. To teach X3 progression from center to forward play, from weakside zoning responsibilities to strongside denial, from center to guard play.
3. To teach good one-on-one moves offensively and defensively.
4. To teach good guard, forward, and center defensing.
5. To teach defensive conditioning.
6. To help develop fast breaks after interceptions.
7. To ease conversion from offensive play to defensive play and from defensive to offensive play.
8. To teach 1 to make good passes to a moving pivot.

9. To teach 3 to receive the ball and be ready for instant fakes and drives on offense.

Procedure:

1. Line players up as shown on the side of the court in Diagram 2-33.
2. Rotate from 1 to 3 to X3 to end of the line. First man in the line becomes the new 1.
3. Player X3 beats 3 to the spot of the intended pass and forces 3 low. You should alter where 1 is stationed daily. X3 should always force 3 away from 1.
4. Player X3 denies 3 the pass in the flash pivot and on out into the corner. If 3 had turned up the court to become a guard, X3 denies pass until 3 gets above 1.
5. We begin the drill by walking through it. We then permit three-quarter speed, and finally full speed. We would allow 3 to stop at the side post and maneuver for the ball, or we would allow him to come to the guard position instead of cutting through the lane into the corner.
6. Now we progress by putting a defensive man on 1 and allowing a two-on-two game after 1 hits 3.
7. Any pass into the pivot should allow for one-on-one immediate maneuvers.
8. After beginning the two-on-two phase, you can progress the drill to full court. If X1 and X3 rebound a missed shot, allow them to fast break. If a steal occurs, allow the defenders to fast break.

Drill 34: Center Help, Yet Recover (3, 4, 5, 6, 7, 8)

Objectives:

1. To teach helping to stop a free-driving forward, yet recovering to play the defensive center position. Defender X5 must not yell "rotate"; X6 is hedging and recovering.
2. To teach recovering on one's own man after hedging. This action takes place in the paint.
3. To teach hustling on inside defense.
4. To teach difference between rotation (Drill No. 55) and hedging and recovering.
5. To teach driving toward the basket from the forward position and being able to pass off to a post player.

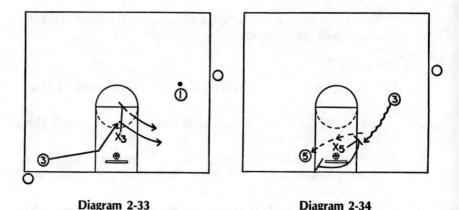

Diagram 2-33   Diagram 2-34

Procedure:

1. Line up players as shown in Diagram 2-34.

2. Rotate from 3 to 5 to X5 to the end of the line. First player in line becomes the new 3.

3. Player 3 fakes, then drives to the basket; X5 must stop him then race to cover 5, who is not permitted to move until after he has received the pass from 3.

4. X5 must really move to get to 5 before he shoots; X5 must not foul 5.

5. We can program the drill for progression. You can give 3 a defender, allowing rotation, hedging, or any of the run-and-jump stunts to be called (this would make it a live two-on-two scrimmage). When you allow this two-on-two scrimmage, your defenders must communicate their intentions; otherwise your defenders will not know the difference between the hedging and the recover techniques, and the rotation techniques; between hedging and recovering, and the run-and-jump stunts.

Drill 35: Helping on the Lob (3, 4, 5, 6)

Objectives:

1. This drill is good for both the zone and the man-to-man defenses. Players must be more alert when playing man-to-man defense because the defender does not have a set area to cover.

2. To teach defense of the lob pass to inside positions.

3. To teach X1 to draw the charge.

4. To teach X1 to help the center (half-man principle) yet handle his own man (full-man principle) when playing man-to-man defense.

5. To teach lob-passing techniques.

6. To teach the center to receive the lob pass without charging.

7. To develop good hands and good inside moves against double-teaming pressure.

Procedure:

1. Line up players as shown in Diagram 2-35.

2. Rotate from 3 to X5 to 5 to X1 to 1 to the end of the line. First man in line becomes the new 3.

3. Player 3 throws lob pass away from defender X5. Player 5 goes to receive the pass while X5 and X1 go for the steal, or X1 draws the charge on 5.

4. Should the pass be successful, X5 must cover 5 and X1 drops back toward the basket to try to stop pass to 1 on backdoor cut—1 does not have to cut backdoor but he logically would. Defender X1 could stay and double-team X5 if that is part of your team defensive plans.

5. Alternate 3's spot on the floor daily. This forces X1 to make a rationally sound judgment; it requires X1 to always see his man and the ball yet offer maximum help inside on 5.

Drill 36: One-on-One Center in the Paint (3, 4, 5, 6)

Objectives:

1. To teach X5 to play continuously on defense inside. X5 must keep excellent defensive positioning.

2. To teach 5 to continuously step toward the passer when receiving a pass. Player 5 immediately goes into a one-on-one move when he receives a pass.

3. To condition offensively and defensively.

4. To teach correct inside passing and receiving.

Procedure:

1. Line players up as shown in Diagram 2-36.

2. Rotate from 1 to 2 to 3 to 4 to 5 to X5 to end of line. First player in line becomes the new 1.

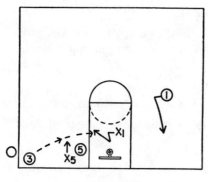

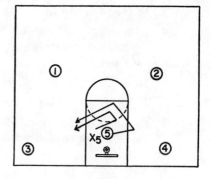

Diagram 2-35   Diagram 2-36

3. Players 1, 2, 3, and 4 all have a basketball; 5 maneuvers toward either 1, 2, 3, or 4. X5 tries to prevent the inside pass, deflecting any pass he can, but keeping position should the ball be completed to 5.

4. When 5 receives a pass, he immediately explodes into a scoring move. X5 tries to prevent the score. Both 5 and X5 try to rebound the made or the missed shot.

5. Player 5 immediately moves toward either 1, 2, 3, or 4 for another pass and another move.

6. Station a manager under the goal to retrieve the made shot. The manager throws the ball back to 1, 2, 3, or 4 (whoever passed the ball inside to 5). This is a tremendous conditioning drill when the balls are kept moving.

7. Allow each attacker and each defender one minute with the offense and one minute with the defense. These two minutes will certainly require stamina from your athletes.

Drill 37: Center Defense with Screeners, Cutters, Posters, and Rollers (3, 4, 5)

Objectives:

1. To teach inside defense.

2. To teach helping out inside, yet recovering to your own assignment.

3. To teach one-on-one inside play, both offensively and defensively.

4. To teach avoiding screens to cover your own man.

5. To teach offensive and defensive rebounding.

6. To teach inside passing from the perimeter.

7. To condition defensively.

Procedure:

1. Line up players as shown in Diagram 2-37.

2. Rotate from offense to defense to end of the line. First three players in line become three new perimeter passers. Three perimeter passers become the new inside attackers.

3. The three inside players may move in any direction they choose. They can screen for each other, roll back to the ball, flash pivot, or make any move to get open. They cannot move more than a step outside the paint.

4. The defenders try to keep the attackers from receiving a pass. Once the attackers receive a pass, the defenders must be ready to stop a shot or another penetrating pass.

5. If the attackers do not like their potential shot, they pass back out to the perimeter and the movement continues.

6. As the ball is passed around the perimeter, each receiver must hold for a two count before passing again.

7. You should allow the defenders to stay on defense for about two minutes. After that, because of the demands of the drill, defensive play becomes weak.

Drill 38: Close the Gap (3, 4, 5)

Objectives:

1. To teach closing the gap—a technique used in both man-to-man and zone defenses.

2. To teach drawing the charge, not blocking.

3. To teach the step-in-and-toward-each-pass helping principle.

Procedure:

1. Line up players to teach them to close the gap from several court positions (Diagrams 2–38 and 2–39).

2. Put a defender on each attacker.

3. At the end of the drill, defensive men rotate to the end of the line, offensive men become defenders, and the next men in line become the new attackers.

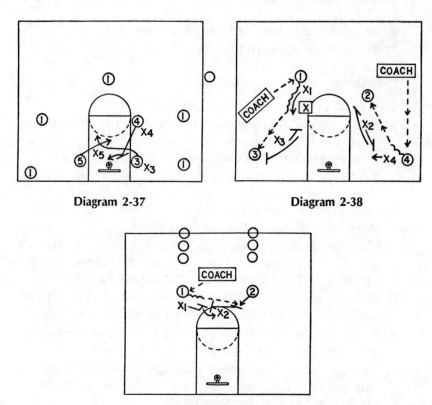

Diagram 2-37   Diagram 2-38

Diagram 2-39

4. Both defensive men are already in an overplay position before the coach tosses the ball. Cut your attackers inside; you can cut them outside if that is your preference.

5. Coach tosses the ball to either offensive man. The attacker immediately begins his drive.

6. The nearest offside defender must get in position to stop the drive. This defender gets both feet on the floor ready to draw the charge. The driver can immediately pass to the open man. Now the defender who closed the gap must use the approach step to recover on his original man. This defender who closed the gap wants to cut the new assignment where there is help (man-to-man) or in a predetermined direction (if you are in a zone). The drill continues until the attacker can drive through the hole for a lay-up. By demanding only lay-ups, you get several closing-the-gaps maneuvers in one drill sequence.

Drill 39: Point-Wing Defense (3, 4, 5)

Objectives:

1. To teach X1 and X3 to react on passes. Defender X3 denies when playing man-to-man; X3 could start at lane position when playing a zone.
2. To teach X1 proper method of covering a vertical-flash-pivot cutter.
3. To teach 1 to become a vertical cutter.
4. To teach 1 and 3 good passing techniques.
5. To teach proper backdoor coverage when X3 is denying.

Procedure:

1. Line up players on side of the court as shown in Diagram 2-40.
2. Rotate from 1 to X1 to 3 to X3 to end of line. First man in line becomes the new 1.
3. Player 1 passes to 3, and X3 and X1 react. 3 is a high wingman, not a corner player.
4. Player 1 cuts vertically, hoping to get a give and go (A) or a backdoor (B); 1 is not to cut behind 3.
5. Player 1 becomes a flash pivot from out front. If 1 chooses the give-and-go route, he is a side pivot. If 1 goes the backdoor route, he can rebreak into the flash-pivot area from the side opposite the ball; X1 should step in and toward each pass as indicated by (A) and (B).

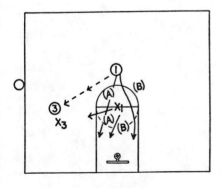

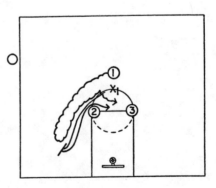

Diagram 2-40   Diagram 2-41

Drill 40: Getting over the Top (3, 4, 5)

Objectives:

1. To teach X1 to avoid picks and to fight over the top of screens when the ball is involved.
2. To teach 1 to dribble his man into a pick or a screen.
3. To teach 1 to jump shoot over a screen.
4. To teach 2 and 3 how to roll without taking their eyes off of the ball, yet be aware of charging.

Procedure:

1. Line up all players in one line on the side of court as shown (Diagram 2-41).
2. Rotate 1 to X1, X1 to 2, 2 to 3, and 3 to the end of the line. The new 1 comes from the front of the line.
3. Player 1 is to dribble until he runs X1 into 2 or 3. Player 1 can go in either direction; it keeps X1 honest.
4. If X1 goes behind 2 or 3, 1 shoots a jump shot over the screen.
5. If X1 gets rubbed off on 2 or 3, 1 can drive to the basket or pass to 2 or 3 on a screen-and-roll play for a lay-up.
6. Players 2 and 3 are not allowed to move to set picks.
7. You could put defenders on 2 and 3; then you could allow switching, jump switching, and so on. Defenders could learn to defense the screen-and-roll maneuver.

3

Man-to-Man
Defensive Drills

In the early days of basketball, only man-to-man defensive teams reached the final four in the NCAA's and in most high school tournaments. Most coaches have grown up feeling that the development of their man-to-man defense was their first defensive priority. That thinking, to a large extent, still prevails today.

To develop your man-to-man to its fullest potential, turn to the page of defensive drills and pick out all the drills marked with the number 3. Those drills are progressive, and, after having taught them, you will have a complete man-to-man defense, including stunts and change-ups. All drills in this chapter are a must for any man-to-man team defense.

There are two ways to teach your man-to-man: Cut the ball to the inside, or cut the ball to the baseline. Both have merit. And both are covered in all these drills. Where there needs to be adjustments made in a drill, we explain how to alter the drill to make it work for cutting the attack outside; all drills are explained for cutting the attack inside.

Drill 41: Ball-You-Man Drill (3, 4, 5)

Objectives:

1. To teach ball-you-man relationships.
2. To teach the defender to see the ball and his man at all times.
3. To teach the defender to always form the flat triangle (man defense).
4. To teach defender to move his head so he can spot any cutter into his area (zone defense).

Procedure:

1. Line players up as shown in Diagram 3-1.
2. Every player should be on the floor. Rotate in each group of threes by going from X1 to 1 to 2 to X1.
3. Player 1 passes to 2 and takes three steps. Player X1 must adjust his positioning so he can see both 1 and the ball; X1 must be between 1 and 2.
4. Player 2 tosses the ball back to 1. Player X1 gets his proper position on 1, the ball handler; 1 passes to 2 and takes two steps. Defender X1 adjusts his position again; 2 then tosses the ball back to 1.
5. Player X1 gets his proper position on 1; 1 passes to 2 and cuts. Player X1 must play proper position defense on 1's cut.
6. The players rotate and the drill continues.

Drill 42: Driver with Helper Shooting, or Cutting Backdoor or Behind (3)

Objectives:

1. To teach hedging.
2. To teach defensive visual reaction.
3. To teach offensive passing and cutting under extreme pressure.
4. To teach the approach step: X2 helps X1 but recovers on 2 as pass is thrown. Player 2 can stay and shoot, or he can drive; 2 can cut behind 1, or go backdoor.
5. To teach double-teaming tactics.
6. To teach the man-and-a-half principle or help and recovery.

Procedure:

1. Line up two attackers and two defenders. Alternate starting spots on the court. Rotate from offense to defense to end of the line. First men in each line become the new attackers.
2. Coach passes to 1. Player 1 drives. X2 hedges and must close the gap if 1 continues his drive (Diagram 3-2).
3. Player X2 should make defensive fakes (hand, head, shoulder, and feet) to slow 1 down or make him stop.

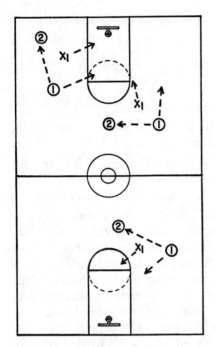

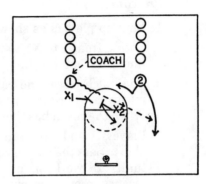

Diagram 3-2

Diagram 3-1

4. Should 1 pass to 2, X2 races in his shuffle steps back to cover
   2 while X1 assumes the help position (stepping in and toward each pass).

5. You can sometimes allow X1 and X2 to double-team with
   another defender, say X3, shooting the gap for a steal. We
   also allow X2 to hedge, then gamble on stealing the pass to 2.

Drill 43: Helping on High Post (3, 4, 5)

Objectives:

1. To teach guards the man-to-man and zone principle of stepping in and toward every pass.

2. To teach defensive center footwork on high-post man (we go
   behind the high post).

3. To teach the defensive principle of sinking on penetrating
   passes and forcing the ball back out (called "diving").

4. To teach quick one-on-one reaction moves by the offensive
   center.

5. To teach defense of quick one-on-one high-post moves.

6. To teach defensive visual reaction: movement as the guard passes the ball.

Procedure:

1. Line up players as shown in Diagram 3-3.

2. Rotate from 1 to X1 to 2 to X2 to 5 to X5 to the end of the line. First man in line becomes the new 1.

3. The coach tosses the ball to either 1 or 2; X1, X2, and X5 must react to correct positioning as the ball is being passed. When the coach has the ball, X5 should be directly behind 5.

4. Players 1 and 2 pass the ball back and forth until they are able to pass the ball inside. This gives your guards an opportunity to work on passing techniques and form. It also teaches proper passing techniques to the center and it teaches the center to learn good reception techniques. When 5 receives the pass, he makes a one-on-one offensive move against X5. Player 5 must make a quick move because either X1 or X2, or both, will sink on the penetrating pass, trying to force the ball back out (the Dive Drill, Drill 53).

5. When X1 or X2 dive (sag on 5), 1 or 2 can cut backdoor. Defenders X1 and X2 must recover.

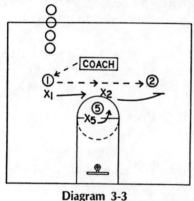

Diagram 3-3

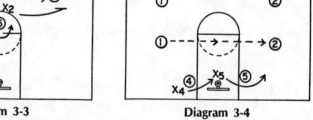

Diagram 3-4

Drill 44: Center-Center Drill (3, 4, 5)

Objectives:

1. To teach inside double-low-post defense against all possible individual double-low post maneuvers.

2. To teach inside posting-up offensively.

3. To teach defense of the lob pass yet recovery on a flash-pivot cutter.

4. To teach fronting low post, three-quartering low post, or playing behind the low post.

5. To teach defensive visual reactions.

Procedure:

1. Line players up as shown in Diagram 3-4.

2. Rotate from 1 to 4 to X4 to end of opposite line. Rotate from 2 to 5 to X5 to end of the opposite line. First man in each line becomes the new 1 and the new 2.

3. Begin the drill by letting 1 and 2 pass back and forth holding the ball for a two count. This forces X4 and X5 to react from strongside defense to helping-side defense.

4. In the beginning, do not allow 4 or 5 to move. After X4 and X5 are visually reacting to the ball, allow 1 and 2 to try to pass inside to the posting 4 and 5.

5. When 2 has the ball, X5 three-quarters (or fronts) 5. X5 gets help from X4 on the side away from X5. Any bounce pass inside should be intercepted. When 1 has the ball, X4 denies 4 the ball and X5 helps.

6. After a few days, allow 1 or 2 to throw a lob pass into either 4 or 5. The weakside defender, X4 or X5, is responsible to deflect this lob. The strongside keeps any direct pass from going inside.

7. After a few days of stopping the lob pass, you can advance the drill by allowing the weakside attacker to flash to the ball. This means the weakside defender must deny the lob, help on direct passes inside, and yet recover sufficiently so he can keep any pass away from his man on the flash-pivot cut.

8. You can then advance to allowing 4 and 5 to screen for each other (see Diagram 3-5 and the accompanying drill—Drill 45).

Drill 45: Center-Center Roll Back (3, 4, 5)

This drill is a continuation of Drill 44 above.

Objectives:
1. To teach inside defenders to stop the screen and roll back to the ball.

2. To teach inside defenders to stop the lob pass.

3. To teach fronting, three-quartering, and playing behind the low post.

4. To teach zoning and denial principles.

Procedure:

1. Line up players as shown in Diagram 3-5.

2. Rotate from 1 to 4 to X4 to end of the opposite line. Rotate from 2 to 5 to X5 to end of the opposite line. First man in each line becomes the new 1 or the new 2.

3. You can do all the different parts of Drill 44 before beginning to screen and roll back.

4. You can defense the screen and roll back two different ways. The method you choose should be consistent coverage for the other parts of your defense:

   A. You can switch on all screens away from the ball. This means X4 and X5 will switch the screen and roll back.

   B. You can have X5 take a step up and slide over the top of X4's screens. X4 zones the area near the big block for a one count. This allows X5 to recover on 5 and X4 to recover on 4. This method allows the assigned defender to stay with his assignment. It means you do not intend to switch on screens away from the ball.

5. Should 1 hit 5 along the baseline, 5 and X5 can go one-on-one. Player 4 can break toward the basket and try to post up X4 or try to get a lob pass on X4.

6 Should 1 hit 4 along the high-side-post area, 5 and 4 can execute the "hi-lo" maneuver. This requires X5 to deny 5 the direct pass and the lob pass (he has no weakside help).

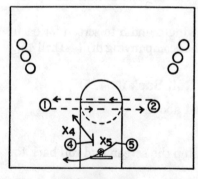

Diagram 3-5

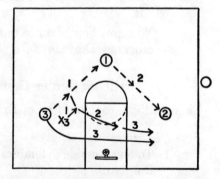

Diagram 3-6

7. If nothing materializes, 4 can slide across the lane and the inside two-on-two drill continues.

Drill 46: Proper Body-Positioning Drill (3)

Objectives:

1. To teach X3 how to contain a one-on-one player.
2. To teach X3 proper sags.
3. To teach X3 to deny and to contest passes.
4. To teach X3 flash-pivot defense.
5. To teach defense of the backdoor cut.
6. To teach 3 how to cut to free himself for different types of passes.
7. To teach one-on-one defensive and offensive play.
8. To teach proper weakside and strongside body positioning.

Procedure:

1. Line up players as shown in Diagram 3-6.
2. Rotate from 2 to 1 to 3 to X3 to end of the line. First player in line becomes the next 2.
3. Player 3 passes to 1 who passes to 2; 3 does not move until 2 has received the pass from 1.
4. Defender X3 guards 3 when he has the ball; X3 denies the pass back to 3 once 3 has passed to 1. Defender X3 sags into the middle of the court when 1 passes to 2.
5. Player 3 flash pivots as 2 receives the pass; X3 must deny the flash pivot.
6. If 3 cannot receive the pass in the flash pivot area, 3 continues into the corner. Defender X3 contests this corner pass to 3; 3 can, of course, go backdoor to try to free himself.
7. Once 3 receives the pass from 2, 3 and X3 go one-on-one.
8. You can alter the drill by allowing 3 to drive on X3 in the beginning.
9. You can, in the beginning, play as though 3 has lost his dribble. This would mean X3 would really be pressuring 3.
10. You should not allow 3 to take a bad shot. He can always pass back outside and begin to try to get the ball back. You should in the early stages of the drill limit the number of dribbles 3 can take.

Drill 47: Wing-Wing Contesting Drill (3)

Objectives:

1. To teach contesting passes to wing attackers.
2. To teach defense of the backdoor cut by wing attackers.
3. To teach the offensive dip to get open.
4. To teach flash-pivot defense.
5. To teach two-on-two offensive and defensive basketball.
6. To teach the backdoor cut.

Procedure:

1. Line players up as shown in Diagram 3-7.
2. Rotate from offense to defense to end of the opposite line. First players in each line become the next attackers.
3. Coach begins the drill by passing to either 2 or 3. In Diagram 3-7, the coach passed to 2.
4. You can allow 2 to attack immediately or you can add the flash-pivot drill (Drill 33). To add the flash-pivot drill, you require 3 to flash pivot when 2 receives the pass.
5. Defender X3 must deny 3 the flash pivot. When 2 hits 3, you begin a live two-on-two anything-goes drill. If 2 cannot hit 3 in three seconds or less, 2 passes back to the coach and 3 returns to his position and the drill continues.
6. Player 3 could cut into the corner after flash pivoting. This would require X3 to deny the flash pivot and to contest the penetrating corner pass.

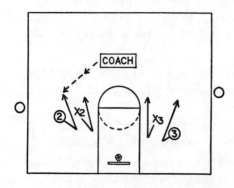

Diagram 3-7

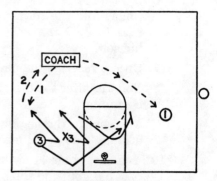

Diagram 3-8

Drill 48: Contest Then Deny Flash Pivot (3)

Objectives:

1. To teach defenders to contest the vertical penetrating pass.
2. To teach defenders to deny the flash pivot.
3. To teach defenders to quickly convert from a strongside defender to a weakside defender.
4. To teach a defender to play one-on-one defense at the corner or wing position.
5. To teach a defender to play one-on-one defense at the high-post position.
6. To teach offensive players to free themselves from denial defense.
7. To teach offensive players how to flash pivot.
8. To teach offensive players one-on-one moves from the corner and from the high post.

Procedure:

1. Line up players as shown in Diagram 3-8.
2. Rotate from 1 to 3 to X3 to end of the line. First man in line becomes the new 1.
3. Defender X3 denies 3 the pass; 3 can then go backdoor or use any of the moves he needs to free himself. When the coach successfully completes a pass to 3, 3 squares up to go one-on-one on X3. But, in the beginning, 3 throws the ball back out to the coach, and 3 begins again to try to free himself. After several completions to 3, the coach throws the ball to 1.
4. Now X3 becomes a weakside defender. Player 3 waits for a two count before flash pivoting toward the ball. Defender X3 must deny this flash pivot.
5. Should 3 successfully receive the pass from 1, 3 and X3 play one-on-one.
6. You could alter the drill by immediately allowing 3 to attack X3 with two dribbles from his corner position. If 3 cannot get a good shot (you determine what is a good shot for your players), 3 passes back to the coach and begins to free himself again. By limiting 3 to one or two dribbles, 3 will have to pass back to the coach frequently. This would

allow the coach to pass to 1 to complete the second phase of the drill. It also allows many denials during each phase of the drill.

Drill 49: Forward Stops Ball Then Recovers (3, 4, 5)

Objectives:

1. To teach X3 to close the gap yet recover to his own man.
2. To teach X3 how to stop a driver who has already taken a few dribbles.
3. To teach 1 to drive and to pass off the drive, almost a lost offensive art.
4. To teach good offensive and defensive one-on-one corner play.
5. To teach X3 to hedge.
6. To teach X3 the approach step.

Procedure:

1. Line up players on the side of the court as shown in Diagram 3-9.
2. Rotate from 1 to 3 to X3 to the end of the line.
3. Player 1 drives to the basket until X3 cuts him off.
4. Player 1 passes to 3; 3 cannot move until he receives the pass, at first. Later we allow 3 to go backdoor or cut behind 1.
5. Defender X3 must hustle back to cover 3 and play him one-on-one.
6. If 1 leaves his feet to pass to 3, X3 can draw the charge if he is in proper position to draw the charge.

Drill 50: Help and Recover: Forward (3, 4, 5)

Objectives:

1. To teach weakside defensive forward his helping responsibilities. Defender X4 must help the strongside forward on backdoor cuts; X4 must draw the charge or deflect the pass.
2. To teach weakside forward to recover after helping. Defender X4 must hustle back to his own man, 4.
3. To teach one-on-one offensive and defensive play.
4. To teach defensive team stunts (run and jump, force backdoor and shoot the gap, etc.) if they are part of your system.

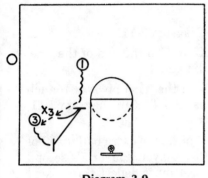

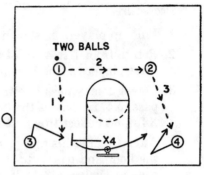

Diagram 3-9	Diagram 3-10

Procedure:

1. Line up players as shown in Diagram 3-10.
2. Rotate from 3 to 1 to 2 to 4 to X4 to the end of the line. First player in line becomes the new 3.
3. Player 1 has an extra ball at his feet. On a given signal, 3 breaks toward 1 but goes backdoor; 1 passes to 3. Defender X4 must deflect this pass or draw the charge (pass 1 in Diagram 3-10). Defender X4 can work a stunt if the defensive plans for the team call for it.
4. Player 1 immediately picks up the second ball and passes to 2 who quickly passes to 4. Defender X4 must recover and deflect or contest this pass to 4.
5. When the pass is completed to 4, X4 and 4 go one-on-one.
6. A manager should retrieve the deflected pass from 1 to 3.
7. If the pass is completed to 3, 3 and X4 go one-on-one. After a score or a defensive rebound, the same players would then repeat the drill.
8. You can make this drill even more lively by also letting 2 have two balls and putting a defender on 3 (say X3). Then you could require 3 and 4 to get open or cut backdoor.

Drill 51: Help and Recover: Center (3, 4, 5)

Objectives:

1. To teach inside defenders to help out inside yet recover to their own man.
2. To teach the lob pass.
3. To teach correct inside-passing techniques.

Procedure:

1. Line up players as shown in Diagram 3-11.
2. Rotate from 1 to 4 to X4 to X5 to 5 to the end of the line. First player in line becomes the new 1.
3. Player 1 may pass to either 4 on the flash pivot or the lob pass to 5. He passes the lob pass to 5 first in Diagram 3-11; X4 must deflect this first pass.
4. After 1 makes his first pass, he picks the extra ball up off of the floor and passes to the other player. Player 1's second pass in Diagram 3-11 is to 4. X4 must deflect this second pass.
5. Anytime a pass is completed to either 4 or 5, they attack X4 and X5 two-on-two.
6. You can alter the drill by putting another guard, 2, outside. Players 1 and 2 pass the ball until one of them passes inside (the lob to the center or the direct pass to the flash pivot). This would require both 1 and 2 to have an extra ball on the floor at their feet. It would also require some rule which would keep 4 and 5 moving from low post to flash pivot. A good rule: In Diagram 3-11, if there is no completed pass to 4 or a lob to 5, 4 rolls back to his initial low-post position as 1 passes to 2 and 5 flash pivots toward 2.

Drill 52: Deny Flash—Help Baseline Drill (3, 4, 5)

Objectives:

1. To teach X1 to deny the flash pivot.
2. To teach X1 his "rotation" responsibilities (see Drill 55), whether man-to-man or a zone.
3. To teach one-on-one offensive and defensive play.

Procedure:

1. Line up players as shown in Diagram 3-12.
2. Rotate from 2 to 1 to X1 to end of the line. First player in line becomes the next 2.
3. Player 1 flash pivots, and X1 denies 1 the ball. Coach throws ball in the direction of 1. Defender X1 deflects it. If 1 should receive the pass, X1 and 1 go one-on-one.
4. You or an assistant coach immediately picks up the extra ball off the floor and passes to 2 after X1 and 1 have gone

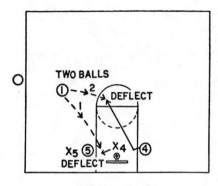

Diagram 3-11

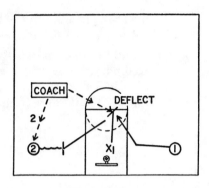

Diagram 3-12

one-on-one or X1 has deflected the pass. Player 2 immediately drives for a basket. Defender X1 must get back to stop the breakaway dribbler 2 (see Rotation Drill, Drill 55).

5. Players 2 and X1 go one-on-one.

Drill 53: Proper Dive Drill (3, 4, 5, 6)

Objectives:

1. To teach defenders on the perimeter to dive inside and force penetrating passes back out.

2. To teach proper team defense on the strong side, the side of the ball.

3. To teach proper pressure positioning and coverage by X3 and X5.

4. To teach the offensive techniques used to combat the denial pressure defense.

Procedure:

1. Line up players as shown in Diagram 3-13.

2. Rotate from 1 to X1 to 3 to X3 to 5 to X5 to end of the line. First player in line becomes the new 1.

3. Player 1 has the ball but has lost his dribble.

4. Player 1 can pass to either 3 or to 5. Both 3 and 5 maneuver to try to get free to receive a pass. You can progress the drill by letting 3 and 5 exchange positions by screening or using some other team offensive move.

5. No lob passes are permitted at first; we then progress the drill by allowing lob passes after mastering the first stage.

You can place X4 in the lane to help on lob passes. Defender X4 would represent a weakside deep defender.

6. Should 1 try to pass inside to 5, X3 would help X5 defend 5. Defender X1 would dive to force the ball back outside. Should 3 pass the ball inside, X1 would help X5 defend 5, and X3 would dive to force the pass back outside.

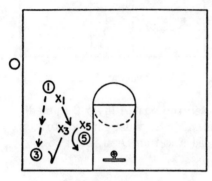

Diagram 3-13

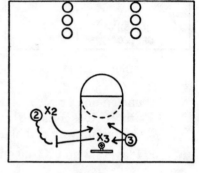

Diagram 3-14

Drill 54: Two-on-Two Rotation (3, 4, 5, 6, 7, 8, 9)

Objectives:

1. To teach attackers to drive hard when they gain an advantage on their defender.
2. To teach weakside defenders to recognize when a dribbler breaks free and is driving toward the basket for a potential lay-up. The weakside deep defender must "rotate" to stop this score.
3. To teach proper defensive rotation.
4. To teach a run-and-jump technique, a hedging maneuver, or some other stunt; and the difference between the run and jump, hedging, and proper rotation.
5. To teach aggressive offensive and defensive play.

Procedure:

1. Line up players as shown in Diagram 3-14.
2. Rotate from offense to defense to the end of the line. First player in each of the two lines becomes the next attacker.
3. Begin the drill by allowing one attacker an advantage so he can drive to the basket. Let the defenders rotate properly.

When the attackers score or are stopped by the defenders, begin again by letting the other attacker gain an advantage.

4. If the rotation is successful, allow the players to play a two-on-two game.

5. When X3 sees that X2 cannot recover onto 2 before 2 turns the corner, X3 must race over to stop 2's drive. Defender X3 should stop 2 outside the paint. If 2 slows down, X3 can call "hedge" and recover on his own assignment. If X3 must pick up 2, X3 yells "rotate" and the rotation drill begins. If you consider the run and jump, X3 could yell "jump" or "trap" and you could be teaching this phase of your team defense.

Drill 55: Zone and Man Rotation Drill (3, 4, 5, 6, 7, 8, 9)

Objectives:

1. Rotation is a key to the success of any team defense. It is used to switch to a momentarily free driving attacker near the basket.

2. To teach visual concentration and reaction.

3. To teach rotation, covering open man from the basket out.

4. To teach channeling the driver who is free: Defender X2 should cut 1 back toward the middle of the court after X2 has rotated.

5. To teach the defenders to "read" and "think" defensively.

6. To teach proper trapping techniques if you intend to trap out of your team defense.

7. To teach difference between hedging, rotation, and the run-and-jump maneuvers.

Procedure:

1. Line up players as shown in Diagram 3-15.

2. Rotate from 1 to X1 to 2 to X2 to 3 to X3.

3. The man who receives the pass is to drive immediately to the basket, 1 in Diagram 3-15.

4. The defender on the pass receiver is to let the offensive player drive with only token defense in the beginning. Later, after denial pressure has been learned, players can go at it under live conditions.

5. The defensive players are to read the situation and rotate

their coverage. The weakside deep man picks up the driver, yelling "rotate." He wants to get to the attacker before the attacker reaches the paint, the lane area. This deep defender makes his judgment based on whether the attacker has gained an advantage as he turns the corner. The weakside outside defender drops to protect the basket area. In Diagram 3-15, X2 takes 1; X3 drops to cover 2. Defender X1 hustles to cover 3. You never want more than a three-man rotation in this area, but you would want to show your players how the three men would rotate even when you are in a five-on-five situation.

6. Start the drill by requiring the offensive men without the ball remain stationary; then begin to let them move, finally going to a three-on-three with anything goes; finally add the rotation drill to your other live drills.

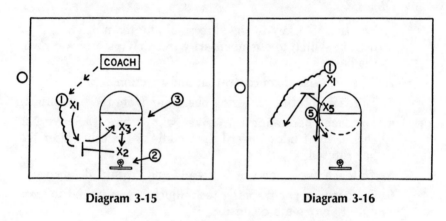

Diagram 3-15   Diagram 3-16

Drill 56: Aggressive Jump Switch Inside (3)

Objectives:

1. To teach a center to jump switch aggressively rather than passively.

2. To teach the perimeter defender to quickly reestablish proper position on the rolling center.

3. To teach a center to try to help a perimeter defender who has been beaten (called hedging) but using jump-switch techniques instead of "rotation" techniques.

4. To teach the perimeter player proper dribbling techniques under extreme defensive pressure.

5. To teach the screener, 5, to use his body properly to shield off X1 for a return pass.

Procedure:

1. Line up players as shown in Diagram 3-16.
2. Rotate from 1 to X1 to 5 to X5 to the end of the line. First player in line becomes the new 1.
3. Player 1 drives toward the basket trying to use 5 as a screen; 1 continues his dribble until he rubs X1 off on 5.
4. Defender X5 "jump switches" to cover 1, while X1 switches to pick up the rolling 5.
5. Defender X5 must call "switch," not "rotate." Of course, if trapping or run and jumping are two of your team techniques, you could add "jump" or "trap" calls.

Drill 57: Teaching the Aggressive Jump Switch (3)

Objectives:

1. To teach the aggressive jump switch.
2. To teach the weakside to help on the screen-and-roll offensive maneuvers.

Procedure:

1. Line up three attackers and three defenders.
2. Rotate from offense to defense to end of each line.
3. In Diagram 3-17, 1 passes to 2 and goes to screen on the ball; after 1 screens, he rolls to the basket.
4. Defender X1 jumps up into the path of the dribbling 2. If you are really an aggressive defensive coach, you can allow X1 and X2 to double-team the dribbler. This means X3 must cover two defenders tightly inside with intentions of planning a run-and-jump shooting of the gap.
5. Defender X1 yells "switch." X2 hustles to get back to proper defensive position on the rolling 1.
6. Player 2 must drive outside X1, or he will charge X1. Should 2 pick up his dribble, he can pass to 3 or wait until 1 comes back outside the lane. If 2 picks up his dribble, all defenders should activate the Team Turnover Drill (Drill 63).
7. Player 2 can reverse his direction and try to drive outside.

This might, should 2 dribble free of X1, require activating the rotation drill (Drill 55).

8. When 2 passes to 1 or to 3, he goes to screen on the ball and another jump switch occurs. Anytime there is a successful backdoor cut, a proper rotation drill should immediately begin.

9. You can include fast breaks off of steals or defensive rebounds. This requires players to play full-court and increases defensive stamina.

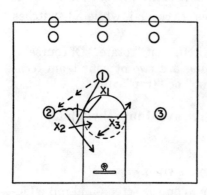 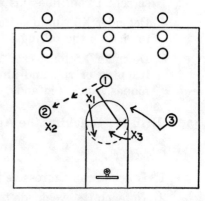

Diagram 3-17   Diagram 3-18

Drill 58: Sliding thru Screens Away from the Ball (3)

Objectives:

1. To teach defenders to stay with their assignments on screens away from the ball.

2. To teach the correct sag: to keep the body in proper position always. To keep proper eye position (on man and ball) when playing weakside defense. If the defender on the weakside sees both man and ball, he should have no trouble avoiding the screen.

Procedure:

1. Line up three attackers and three defenders (Diagram 3-18).

2. Player 1 passes to 2 and 1 goes to screen for 3. Defender X3 should use peripheral vision and see the screen developing.

3. Defender X1 sags toward the basket as 1 goes away from the ball.

4. Player X3 takes a step back toward the basket and slides through the screen, hoping for an interception on a pass from 2 to 3.

5. Player 2 passes to 3 who passes to 1 and the defense continues to slide through the screens.

6. After teaching the aggressive jump-switch drill (Drill 57) and the defense of the backdoor cut, you can allow the offense to screen on the ball, screen away from the ball, or cut backdoor, making it a live three-on-three defensive drill.

Drill 59: Hedging—Fighting over the Tops of Screens (3)

Objectives:

1. To teach the defensive center the hedging technique: the ability to force a driver out wider than the screen, allowing the driver's defender to fight over the top. Diagram 3-19 shows the forward-center hedging drill, and Diagram 3-20 displays the guard-center hedging drill.

2. To teach the defensive forward (or guard) to fight over the top of any screen where the dribble is involved.

3. To teach the dribbler to drive his man by dribbling into a stationary screen; then to shoot the jump shot over the screen or to drive around the screen for the lay-up.

4. To teach good ball handling under extreme pressure.

5. To teach good defensive timing and communication between the defender on the dribbler and the defensive center.

Procedure:

1. Line players up as shown in Diagrams 3-19 and 3-20.

2. Rotate from 3 to X3 to 5 to X5 to the end of the line (Diagram 3-19). Rotate from 1 to X1 to 5 to X5 to 4 to X4 to the end of the line (Diagram 3-20). The first man in line becomes the new dribbler.

3. The dribbler is to drive his defensive man into 5. Player 5 is not permitted to move. The dribbler keeps his dribbling alive until he is successful in rubbing his defender off on 5 (or on 4 in Diagram 3-20).

4. Defender X5 uses his hedging techniques to force the dribbler outside and off his course; X5 must be sure to get out of X3's way (X1 in Diagram 3-20), permitting X3 (or X1) to

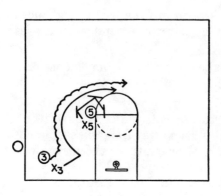 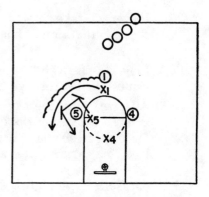

Diagram 3-19   **Diagram 3-20**

catch up to the dribbler. Proper mastery of the footwork involved will assure successful timing between X5 and the dribbler's defender.

5. When the dribbler rubs his man off on the screener, he may jump shoot over the screen or drive to the basket.

6. Never allow the dribbler's defender to slide through—that gives the dribbler the jump shot over the screen. For development of hedging and fighting over the top, you must not allow X5 the aggressive jump switch. But once you are comfortable with your defender's ability to fight over the top while guarding the dribbler, you may want to allow decision making by the two defenders. When you allow the defenders to decide to use the fight over the top or the aggressive jump switch, you should have clearly defined rules for when you want that to occur.

Drill 60: Weakside-Guard Drill (3, 4, 5)

Objectives:

1. To teach X1 to help on passes into the center lane yet be able to recover on his own man (man-to-man) or to his area (zone).

2. To teach good one-on-one defensive and offensive play.

3. To teach X1 to sink in and toward every pass principle (man) or to sag the three-step drill to the inside (zone).

4. To teach hustling defense.

5. To teach correct passing techniques by 2 and 3.

Procedure:

1. Line up players as shown in Diagram 3-21. Rotate from 1 to 2 to 3 to X1 to the end of the line. First man in line becomes the new 1.

2. Player 1 passes to 2 who passes to 3.

3. Defender X1 sinks one step in and toward every pass.

4. Player 3 has an extra ball at his feet.

5. When the first ball gets to 3, he passes toward the center of the lane, then 3 quickly picks up the extra ball and passes to 2 who passes to 1.

6. X1 must deflect pass into the center court, then recover enough to get to 1 by the time he receives the other pass.

7. X1 and 1 go one-on-one. If you are teaching your man-to-man defense, you should require X1 to channel 1 in the direction mandated by your defensive team principles. The same is true if you are teaching your zone.

Drill 61: Weakside Combination-Cut Drill (3)

Objectives:

1. To teach weakside defenders their responsibilities in defending different types of cuts.

2. To teach attackers away from the ball how and when to cut to the ball.

Procedure:

1. Line up players as shown in Diagram 3-22.

2. Rotate from 1 to X1 to 3 to X3 to 2 to the end of the line. First player in line becomes the next 1.

3. Defender X1 cuts the dribbler, 1, toward the 28-foot hashmark. When 1 reaches the 28-foot marker, X1 cuts him inside. Player 1 passes to the coach who immediately passes to 2; 1 cuts down the lane to the low post. Defender X1 must jump in the direction of the pass. This gives X1 the proper ball-defense-man position on the cut.

4. When 1 reaches the low post, 1 tries to post up X1. Player 2 must toss the lob pass to 1; X3 must deflect this lob pass.

5. Meanwhile, 2 has picked up the extra ball and passed to the

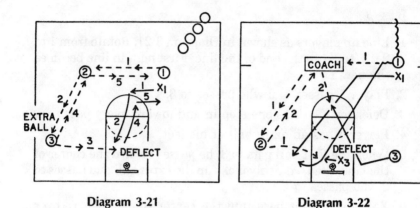

Diagram 3-21   Diagram 3-22

coach. This cues 3 to flash pivot toward the coach; X3 must recover to prevent 3 from receiving the pass.

6. You can change the drill by having the coach toss the first pass to 3 on the flash pivot; X3 must deflect his pass then pick up the second basketball and pass to 2. Player 2 tosses the lob pass to the cutting 1; X3 must deflect this lob.

Drill 62: Stunting the Reverse Dribbler (3)

Objectives:

1. To help defenders learn what a man-to-man defensive stunt is.

2. To teach X1 to force 1 to use a reverse dribble.

3. To teach X2 to recognize the dribbling reverse and then to apply double-teaming or run-and-jump mechanics.

4. To teach X3 to shoot the gap at the exact moment of the reverse.

5. To teach defensive teamwork on full- and half-court stunts.

6. To teach drawing the charge.

7. To teach 1 good one-on-one offensive moves, how to avoid the defensive double-team, and how to handle the run-and-jump stunts.

Procedure:

1. Line up players as shown in Diagram 3-23.

2. Rotate from 1 to X1 to 2 to X2 (to X3 when he is in the drill) to the end of the line. First player in line becomes the new 1.

3. Player 1 goes one-on-one against X1; 1 tries to score.

4. Player X2 sags off his man one and one-half step toward the ball and is looking for the opportunity to double-team.

5. As long as 1 tries to score by facing X1, all X2 can do is sag and hedge, but should 1 run a dribbling reverse, turning his back to the defensive player, X2 immediately goes for the double-team or the run and jump. By requiring X2 to stay out of the play until 1 reverses, you teach X1 to force the reverse and you teach X2 to recognize when the reverse is about to occur.

6. You can use this drill for both half-court and full-court defensive recognition of the dribbling reverse.

7. You can progress the drill by adding X3 who is to shoot the gap on a pass from 1 to 2.

8. You can allow X1 and X2 to run the two-man run-and-jump drill (Drill 124).

9. You should have X2 try to arrive just as 1 comes out of his dribbling reverse. This frequently results in a charging call or a walking violation.

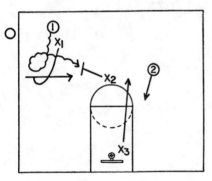

Diagram 3-23

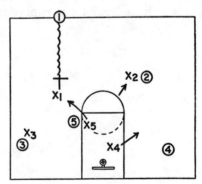

Diagram 3-24

Drill 63: Team Turnover Drill (five-second drill) (3)

Objectives:

1. To teach 1 to dribble under pressure.

2. To teach X1 to halt the dribble; to teach double-teaming or hedging techniques to stop the dribbler, yet recovering to his own man to deny a return pass (to get the five-second call).

3. To teach coverage of the passing lanes so we can force the five-second call.

4. To teach 1 to pass under pressure.

Procedure:

1. Line up five men on offense with five defenders. You can use four attackers and allow the extra defender to double-team the ball handler.

2. Allow 1 to dribble until X1 forces him to stop. We sometimes use five defenders against four attackers, allowing double-teaming of the ball to stop the dribbler. You want to use the rotation rules of your full-court and half-court pressure team defenses; our rule is the container always hustles back to the open man.

3. After the dribbler passes the ball the drill can begin again from the new receiver. Anytime the dribble is killed, all defenders contest the passing lanes to their man, forcing the turnover call after five seconds.

4. Should there be a turnover in the form of a steal, you could have your team run your fast break.

4

Zone Defensive Drills

Most coaches believe they have to teach man-to-man defense before their zone defense can become effective. That erroneous concept prevents coaches from doing more with their zone defenses, from developing many different zone stunts. They simply do not have the time.

While it certainly would not hurt to teach man-to-man defense first, it does not follow that to have an effective zone you have to develop your man-to-man. You do, however, need to develop the fundamentals of Chapter 2, or your zone will never reach championship caliber. All you need to do to develop your zone defense fully is to refer to the page of drills and consider all the drills marked by the number 4.

You could go even deeper into your zone play by specializing: You could choose the 1-2-2, or the 1-3-1, or the 2-3. Then you could limit your drills to the number 4 and the numbers 4A, 4B, or 4C (whichever is applicable). In this chapter, Drills 64–74 will help develop all the zones while Drills 75–79 are specifically for the 2-1-2 or 2-3 zones. Drills 80–89 deal primarily with the teaching of the 1-2-2 zone, but they can also help in developing the 1-3-1. Drills 90–93 are just for the 1-3-1 zone.

Drill 64: Flash-Pivot Reaction Drill (3, 4, 5)

Objectives:

1. To teach quick reactions defensively.
2. To teach defense of the flash pivot.
3. To teach one-on-one play both offensively and defensively.
4. To teach the defender proper body positioning.

Procedure:

1. Line up players as shown in Diagram 4-1.

2. Coach numbers the players to the left of him and to the right of him so that both players immediately to the left and right have the number 1. The next two have the number 2, the next two have the number 3, and so on.

3. Coach tosses the ball to one of the players in the semi-circle. That player becomes the passer. His counter number immediately flash pivots. Player X6 defends the flash pivot. If the flash pivot receives the pass, X6 and the flash pivot go one-on-one.

4. Player X6 stays on defense for several flash pivots. Then X6 takes someone's place (the coach tells who) in the semicircle, and the player X6 replaces becomes the new defender, and X6 takes the number of the player he replaced.

5. Coach should have an extra ball so he can keep X6 moving on defense. In Diagram 4-1, as soon as X6 stops 2, steals the pass, or allows 2 to score, the coach would want to pass again. Player X6 must hustle into proper body position and deny the next flash pivot.

6. You can make the drill highly competitive by requiring X6 to stop two attackers in a row. The last attacker he stops becomes the new X6.

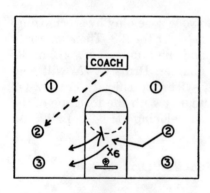

Diagram 4-1

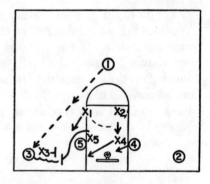

Diagram 4-2

Drill 65: Baseline-Trap Drill (3, 4, 5)

Objectives:

1. Regardless of the zone defense you run, it will always be a 2-3 when the ball is in the corner: Therefore, the objective is to teach trapping techniques when the driver gets free on the baseline.

2. To teach proper slides of your zone defense when there is a defensive breakdown by your zone defenders.

3. To teach post-up defense.

4. To teach posting up and passing inside.

Procedure:

1. Line up five attackers and five defenders as shown in Diagram 4-2. For the purpose of the drill, do not allow defenders to contest the pass from 1 to either 2 or 3.

2. Rotate from offense to defense until all have played their spots on your zone defense.

3. Player 1 can pass to either 2 or to 3, or 1 can pass to 4 and 5 posting up. Players 2 and 3 can pass crosscourt to each other as well as back out to 1.

4. If 2 or 3 can pass inside, they do.

5. When either 2 or 3 can drive the baseline, they are to do so. Defenders must react with the trap and the proper gap-shooting techniques. In Diagram 4-2, 3 drives the baseline. Defender X3 tries to close it but cannot; X5 leaves 5 and helps X3 trap 3. Meanwhile X4 has come over to cover 5. Defender X2 has dropped back to cut off the pass to 4. If 2 had driven the baseline, the rotation would show X4 and X5 trapping 2's baseline drive. Defender X3 would slide over to cover 4; X1 would drop to stop the pass to 5.

6. Both 2 and 3, should nothing develop, have the option to pass back out to 1. You might even allow 4 and 5 to roll to open spots inside the zone instead of posting up.

Drill 66: Wing-Corner Lane-Trap Drill (4, 5)

Objectives:

1. To teach defenders how to lane while playing a zone.

2. To teach defenders how to trap while playing a zone.

3. To teach attackers how to pass correctly when facing a trapping or laning zone.

4. To teach defenders how to shoot the gap.

Procedure:

1. Line up players as shown in Diagrams 4-3 and 4-4.

2. Make sure all defenders in your zone who are responsible

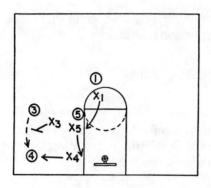

Diagram 4-3   Diagram 4-4

for defensive positions X1, X3, X4, and X5 learn their slides and responsibilities.

3. We use only one side of the offense at a time to teach these slides and traps. Diagram 4-3 shows a laning technique out of the 1-2-2 zone. Diagram 4-4 shows a corner-trapping technique out of the 1-2-2 zone.

4. When a trap is set, X1 must choose between guarding high post (safest trap), guarding 3, or playing between the lane to 3 and 5.

5. Attackers can pass the ball between 1, 3, and 5; but when the pass goes into the corner, X3 decides to lane or trap. Player X1 responds to X3's call.

Drill 67: Channeling the Ball (4, 5)

Objectives:

1. To teach zone defenders how to channel the ball to a most favored position by the defense.

2. To teach the teamwork involved in channeling the ball.

Procedure:

1. Line up four attackers and four defenders as shown in Diagram 4-5.

2. Make sure all potential candidates for X1, X2, X3, and X5 get to drill at those positions.

3. Defensive player X1 plays on right offensive side of 1, facing 1, forcing 1 toward 3; X2 has sagged allowing the pass to 3. But X3 has played in the lane between 1 and 2, discouraging the pass to 2. Usually, during a game situation, 1 will

pass to 3, the line of least resistance. Player X1 denies the pass back to 1 at the top of the circle.

4. Player 3 can pass into the corner to the coach. When this happens, 3 cuts through and fills 2's position, 1 will slide over, filling 3's position, and 2 rotates to the point.

5. Defender X2 denies the pass (lanes it) from the coach back to 1. But should 1 get the pass from the coach and X1 denies the pass back to the top of the circle while X2 channels the pass to the coach. The defense intends to keep the ball on the right side of the court.

6. You can, of course, run this drill to other areas of the court. You should decide where your team defense intends to channel the ball, then drill on impelling the ball to those most favored defensive spots.

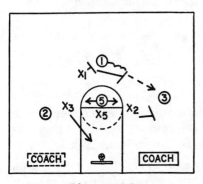

Diagram 4-5

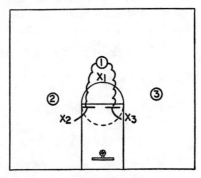

Diagram 4-6

Drill 68: Zone Driving Drill (4, 5, 6)

Objectives:

1. To teach defenders to play a dribbler and not the dribble.
2. To teach defenders nearest the ball to close the gap on drives yet recover to their own area.
3. To teach the slides of your zone defense.

Procedure:

1. Line up players as shown in Diagram 4-6.
2. Make sure you drill all the defenders on the defensive rules from each position. Diagram 4-6 shows the outside three defenders in a 1-2-2 zone. You should have a drill for the right side and for the left side. If your zone is not a 1-2-2,

you should design drills to prevent dribbling penetration from each zone defender's position.

3. Once 1 passes to either 2 or 3, everyone in our rules would sink except the defender on the ball. We cut 2 and 3 outside so no one in this drill could close the gap. But if your zone cuts 2 or 3 inside, you could continue closing the gap as the drill is shown in Diagram 4-6.

4. To continue our coverage, and your coverage should always reflect your zone rules, when 1 passes to 2 or to 3, 2 or 3 would have two dribbles to score. If they cannot score, they pass back to 1 and the drill continues.

5. You could add an X4 and X5 on the big blocks. Players 2 and 3 are cut outside. Defensive players X4 and X5 close the gaps on these drives. If you add a 4 and a 5 in each corner, you could have a continuous closing-the-gap drill from a 1-2-2 zone.

Drill 69: Zone Screen-Rule Drill (4, 5, 6)

Objectives:

1. To teach defenders to avoid screening maneuvers while playing your zone defense. Diagrams 4-7 and 4-8 show the 1-2-2 zone: You should use the zone of your choice.

2. To teach the attackers how and where to screen the zone defenses. This enables your attackers to take advantage of weak defenders as well as the holes inherent in the different zone defenses.

Procedure:

1. Line up players as shown in Diagram 4-7 (baseline defenders) and 4-8 (perimeter defenders).

2. Diagram 4-7 shows a passing drill using a baseline screen, and Diagram 4-8 depicts a perimeter screening drill using the dribble.

3. Begin the drill by not allowing the attackers to shoot. After the defenders have learned the method you wish to use to get over the top of screens or switching it, then you can allow the jump shot.

4. Be sure each candidate for a defensive position gets to play their position in the drill.

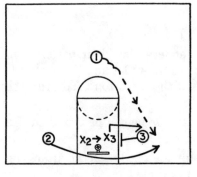

Diagram 4-7   Diagram 4-8

5. In Diagram 4-7, if 2 does not get the baseline shot, 3 posts up then goes to the other side of the lane. Player 2 passes back to 1, and 2 moves back into the lane. Now the drill continues. You can allow 2 or 3 to cut off the other's screen. You need a signal to let the cutters know which is to cut, or you can allow them to post up for a pass directly from 1. You could even allow one of them to break to high post and run the Hi-Lo drill (Drill 87).

6. In Diagram 4-8, 1 dribbles while 2 fills 1's spot. After 3 screens, 3 goes over to fill 2's spot. Anytime there is a shot possibility, have defenders use block-out responsibilities. Anytime players can drive, use drill 38, Close the Gap drill. If nothing results, have 1 pass back to 2 and 2 can drive, activating the Close the Gap drill. Two other possibilities are that 2 can come toward 1's or 3's screen, or 2 can pass to 1 or to 3 and go screen. Initially, 1 could have passed to 2 or to 3 and went to screen on, or away from, the ball.

Drill 70: Cutter's Drill (cover "over") (4, 5)

Objectives:

1. To teach the slides of your zone defense.
2. To teach covering cutters so passes cannot be completed inside.
3. To teach perimeter passing against zones with intent to pass inside.
4. To teach covering over for your match-up zone.
5. To teach defensive communication while playing a zone.

Procedure:

1. Line up players as shown in Diagram 4-9.
2. Make sure all perimeter defenders play their positions in your zone defense. Diagram 4-9 shows X1 and X2 as guards and X3 and X4 as forwards of the 2-1-2 zone. You run the zone of your choice.
3. Any attacker can pass and stay or he can pass and cut. In the beginning allow no shooting.
4. After defenders manage to stay matched with the attackers, you can begin to allow shooting.
5. On outside guard cutting, the guard should go with the cutter to the paint, then he should yell "over," telling his teammates to slide over one man (match-up as well as regular zone).
6. After defenders learn "slide" (Drill 71), they can use either "slide" or "over" to stay matched with the attackers.

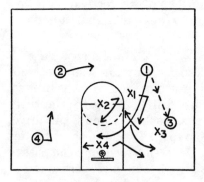
Diagram 4-9

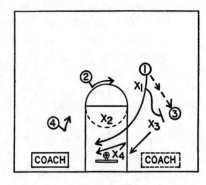
Diagram 4-10

Drill 71: Penn State Sliding-Zone Drill (cover "slide") (4, 5, 6)

Objectives:

1. To teach the slides of your zone defense.
2. To teach covering cutters so passes cannot be completed inside.
3. To teach perimeter passing against zones with intent to pass inside.
4. To teach covering "slide" for your match-up zone.
5. To teach defensive communication while playing a zone.

Procedure:

1. Line up players as shown in Diagram 4-10.
2. Make sure all perimeter defenders play their positions in your zone defense. Diagram 4-10 shows X1 and X2 as guards and X3 and X4 as forwards of a 2-1-2 zone. You run the zone of your choice.
3. Any attacker can pass and stay or he can pass and cut. In the beginning allow no shooting.
4. After defenders manage to stay matched with the attackers, you can allow shooting.
5. At the learning stages a coach should be in either corner so 3 and 4 can pass to the coach and cut. This allows defenders to see the reasons for "slide" maneuvers.
6. On the pass from guard to forward the guard should sink even with the forward and go to the forward with the ball, and call "slide." Upon hearing this, the defensive forward should drop directly to the big block.
7. After the defenders have learned "over" (Drill 70), they can use either "slide" or "over" to stay matched with the attackers.

Drill 72: Deny Flash-Pivot—Defend Post (3, 4, 5)

Objectives:

1. To teach defenders to deny flash pivot.
2. To teach defenders to defend against post-up maneuvers.
3. To teach hustling defense.
4. To teach one-on-one offensive and defensive basketball from high post, low post, and corner positions.

Procedure:

1. Line up players as shown in Diagram 4-11.
2. Rotate from 1 to 2 to 3 to X3 to end of the line. First player in line becomes the next 1.
3. Player 1 has an extra basketball at his feet.
4. Player 3 breaks toward 1. Defender X3 denies the flash pivot maneuver, and deflects 1's pass.
5. Player 1 picks up the extra basketball and throws a pass to 2. Player 3 tries to post up X3; X3 must prevent this post-up maneuvering.

6. Should 1 complete the pass to the flash pivot 3, X3 and 3 play one-on-one. Should 2 get the ball into the posting-up 3, X3 and 3 play one-on-one basketball.

7. To make it competitive you could require X3 to stop 3 at both the high and low post or X3 must go again. This would also make 3 want to score each and every time; otherwise 3 would be the new defender. If 3 should score at both high and low post, you could alternate another 3 into that spot. Rotation of another 3 would also make it more attractive for 3 to score every possession.

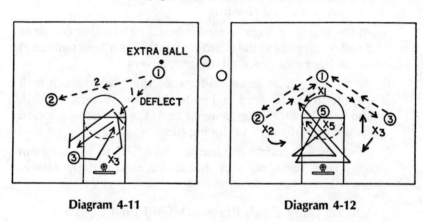

Diagram 4-11   Diagram 4-12

Drill 73: Perimeter Dive—Center Alive (3, 4, 5)

Objectives:

1. To teach a center defender to deny passes inside and get lob-pass help from perimeter man on the weak side.

2. To teach the perimeter slides of your zone defense. Put 1, 2, and 3 where your zone defenders would start (shown in Diagram 4-12 for a 1-3-1 or 1-2-2 zone).

3. To compare perimeter passing to inside passing.

4. To teach the step-in-and-toward-every-pass defensive principle of both the man-to-man and zone defense.

5. To teach coverage of a moving pivot.

6. To teach offensive pivot moves under pressure.

7. To teach offensive and defensive one-on-one center play.

8. To teach sinking and forcing ball back out (perimeter dive).

Procedure:

1. Line up players on side of court as shown in Diagram 4-12.
2. Rotate from 1 to X1 to 2 to X2 to 3 to X3 to 5 to X5 to end of the line. First player in line becomes the new 1.
3. Players 1, 2, and 3 cannot move, but they must pass the ball back and forth until 5 gets open; X5 tries to keep the ball from going inside to 5.
4. Run the drill for about 30 seconds per defender, then rotate.
5. If a pass is completed to 5, he and X5 go one-on-one.
6. Defender X1, X2, and X3 step in and toward every pass.
7. The correct defender, either X1, X2, or X3, must sink and force the penetrating pass back out (perimeter dive).
8. The correct defender, X2 or X3, must help on the lob pass.
9. You can advance the drill by allowing 1, 2, and 3 to drive. This would eliminate X2 and X3 just considering denial of the pass to their assignments. X1, X2, and X3 would now have to close the gaps. If the driver got through the gap, it would require the rotation drill (Drill 55).

Drill 74: Outside Perimeter: Four vs. Three (4, 5)

Objectives:

1. To teach the outside three their proper slides.
2. To teach the outside three how to cover their positions yet help deny passes into the high post.

Procedure:

1. Line players up as shown in Diagram 4-13.
2. Rotate your players from offense to defense to the end of their respective lines. First man in line becomes the next attacker at that position. Make sure each player gets drilled at the position for which they will be responsible.
3. Players 1, 2, and 3 pass the ball around until 2 or 3 can pass inside to 5; 5 then quickly attacks the basket.
4. Anytime 2 or 3 can drive to the inside and get a shot off they may do so: Remember our rule is for the wing men to make the attacker drive to the outside.
5. Anytime 1 can drive around X1, he may do so. Defenders X2 or X3 should close the gap on 1's drive.

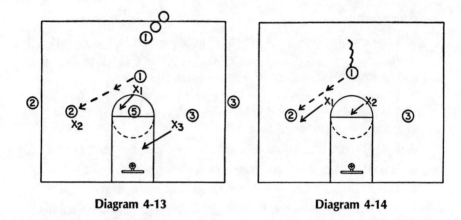

Diagram 4-13   Diagram 4-14

Drill 75: 2-1-2 Two-Guard Drill (4A, 5)

Objectives:

1. To teach two defensive guards to defend three perimeter attackers—a point and two wings.
2. To get the two wings and the point to shoot jump shots quickly.
3. To teach the skip pass.
4. To teach the offensive step-through move.

Procedure:

1. Line up players as shown in Diagram 4-14.
2. Players 1, 2, and 3 attack X1 and X2.
3. Players X1 and X2 must stop 1, 2, and 3 from getting a jump shot away.
4. Players X1 and X2 must force the attackers to dribble in the desired direction of the team defense.

Drill 76: 2-1-2 Inside Defensive Drill (4A, 5)

Objectives:

1. To teach the inside three players their slides in the 2-1-2 or 2-3 zone.
2. To teach X4, X5, and X3 their rebounding positions.
3. To teach defense of post-up maneuvers.

Procedure:

1. Line up players as shown in Diagram 4-15.
2. Players 1 and 2 can shoot jump shots, drive, or pass to 3 or 4.
3. Player 5 can pass into 3 or 4 on post-up maneuvers.
4. Should 1 or 2 drive and you have already taught the trapping of baseline drives (Drill 65), you would want to activate that drill.
5. Begin by requiring that 1, 2, and 5 hold the ball for a two count. After the slides are mastered, let the attackers pass the ball as quickly as they like. This requires real hustling defense.

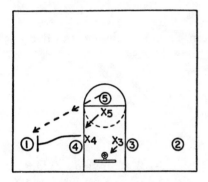

Diagram 4-15

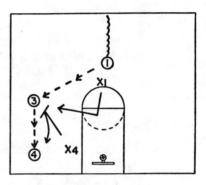

Diagram 4-16

Drill 77: 2-1-2 Strongside Defense (4A, 5)

Objectives:

1. To teach X1 and X4 how to defense three attackers on the ball side.
2. To teach the Penn State sliding-zone defensive maneuver.
3. To teach 1, 3, and 4 to get the quick jump shot off against zone defenders.

Procedure:

1. Line up players as shown in Diagram 4-16.
2. Defender X1 must stop 1's penetration; 1 can pass to either 3 or 4.
3. If the pass goes to 3 and the running distance is too great for

X1 to control, X4 holds 3 until X1 can arrive. When X1 arrives, X4 drops to the big block.

4. If 3 quickly passes to 4, X4 should be able to run between 3 and 4. Either the distance between 3 and 4 must be short enough for X3 to run or the distance between 1 and 3 must be short enough for X1 to run. The measurements of the court dictate this reasoning.

5. Begin by requiring each new receiver to hold the ball for a two count. Advance to allowing quick passing of the ball after the slides have been mastered.

Drill 78: The 2-1-2 Four Perimeter Player Defense (4A, 5)

Objectives:

1. To teach the four perimeter players to defend the five perimeter holes of the 2-1-2 zone defense.
2. To teach the slides of the four perimeter men.
3. To teach hustling zone defense.

Procedure:

1. Line up the players as shown in Diagram 4-17.
2. This is a continuation of the 2-1-2 strongside defensive drill. Defenders X1 and X4 still cover 1, 2, and 4; X2 and X3 will cover 1, 3, and 5.
3. If the ball is reversed or if it originally goes down the other side, X2 and X3 run the 2-1-2 strongside defensive drill.
4. When a shot is taken, have defenders box out in their positions.

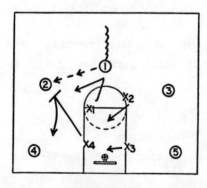

Diagram 4-17

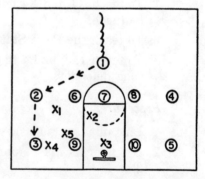

Diagram 4-18

5. If dribbling penetration occurs, activate Closing the Gap (Drill 38) or the Rotation drill (Drill 55).

6. You could even put an X5 in the middle and, should the baseline drive occur, you could activate the Baseline Trap drill (Drill 65). With X5 in the drill, you really have all five defensive men running your defense.

Drill 79: The Fifteen-Man Drill (4A, 5)

Objectives:

1. To show five defenders if they cooperate as a unit, they can cover the ten scoring areas against the 2-1-2 zone.

2. To teach the proper slides of the 2-1-2 zone.

Procedure:

1. Line up ten offensive players as shown in Diagram 4-18.

2. Have 1 bring the ball down the floor and pass to anyone. A defender must cover the receiver before he gets the shot off.

3. No attacker can cut. They can only receive a pass and shoot the jump shot.

4. Defenders must hustle and they must cooperate if they are to stop ten attackers. They must know their slides and they must communicate.

5. Have your defenders run the slides of your 2-1-2 zone. Of course, you can also use this drill even if your intent is a 1-2-2 or a 1-3-1 zone. You may want to change the spots of some of the offensive men so they will be in the holes and the seams of the zone you are teaching.

6. When a shot is taken, be sure your players go to their assigned rebounding positions.

Drill 80: 1-2-2 Front Slides (three cover four) (4B, 5)

Objectives:

1. To teach the perimeter three of the 1-2-2 zone their slides.

2. To teach hustling, aggressive zone defenses rather than developing passive zone defenders.

3. To teach three defenders how they can keep four attackers from scoring by proper slides and teamwork.

Procedure:

1. Line up players as shown in Diagram 4-19.

2. Make sure all potential candidates for three perimeter positions get to drill on those positions.

3. Players 1, 2, 3, and 4 pass the ball around the perimeter. They may use skip passing.

4. Players X1, X2, and X3 must keep up with the ball and prevent a jump shot from occurring.

5. Begin the drill with X1 on the ball (1 in Diagram 4-19). When 1 passes to 2, 1 must hustle to release X3 onto 4. This always keeps a defender on the ball and a defender on the next two immediate pass receivers. This compels a skip pass if an open shot is to occur. However, if the defenders hustle, they can arrive as the skip pass arrives.

6. You can also allow the attacker to drive inside (Closing the Gap drill, Drill 38).

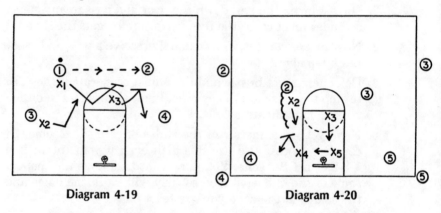

Diagram 4-19   Diagram 4-20

Drill 81: Wings Cut Outside—Baseline Inside (4B, 5)

Objectives:

1. When playing a zone you want to give your people a primary route of coverage. Player X2, in Diagram 4-20, has primary coverage of 2's inside drive; X2, in other words, will force 2 to drive toward the outside if 2 is to drive anywhere. Player X4 will offer help by closing the gap. Should X2 get by the gap-closing techniques, X5 would call "rotation."

2. Player X4 must not give up the baseline drive to his man 4.

3. To teach proper channeling (you may choose other coverages—use the rules of your zone defensive techniques).

4. To teach slides of the zone defense.

5. To teach closing the gap.

6. To teach help and recover.

7. To teach rotation while playing a zone.

Procedure:

1. Line up players as shown in Diagram 4-20.

2. Rotate the outside performers and the inside performers: All rotations are from offense to defense to the end of the line; first man in each line becomes the next attacker. Make sure all defenders play the positions that they will be responsible for.

3. Players 2, 3, 4, and 5 may drive when they receive the ball. Their defenders must make sure if there is a drive it goes in the proper direction: Defenders X4 and X5 cannot give up the baseline; X2 and X3 cannot give up the drive to the inside.

4. When 2 or 3 drive outside, X2 and X3 get closing-the-gap help from X4 and X5; X4 and X5 must learn to hedge yet recover. Players X4 and X5 must communicate their desires to their teammates.

5. When 4 or 5 drive inside, X4 and X5 get closing-the-gap help from X2 and X3. This is not as dangerous a drive as the one by 2 or 3.

6. After closing the gap, each defender must recover back on their own assignment.

7. Should 4 or 5 drive the baseline, X4 and X5 should trap the ball (see Drill 65).

8. Any player can pass to another player at any time. They may pass off a drive, or they may pass without attempting to drive. This makes the drill highly competitive.

9. Should a drive be successful on the strong side, the rotation drill should come into play. Communication is important so all defenders will know the intentions of each player. At the least, the weakside defender should draw a charge on all lay-ups.

Drill 82: Two-Ball Drills—Weakside Wing (4B, 5)

Objectives:

1. To teach the defensive weakside wing his slides of the 1-2-2 zone and of all match-up zone defenses.

2. To teach defensive rebounding.

3. To teach the defensive weakside wing to help out inside yet recover on his own man.

4. To teach hustling defense.

5. To teach one-on-one offensive and defensive play.

6. To condition defensively.

Procedure:

1. Line up players as shown in Diagram 4-21.

2. Rotate from 3 to 5 to X3 to end of the line. First player in line becomes the next 3.

3. A coach and 3 pass back and forth until the coach throws the ball into 5. Defender X3 must deflect this pass to 5. The coach immediately picks up the second ball off the floor and passes to 3; X3 must hurry back out to cover 3. Meanwhile 5 has recovered the deflected pass and passed it back to the manager who lays it at the coach's feet.

4. Player 3 has two dribbles to attack X3. If 3 cannot score in two dribbles, he passes back to the coach and the drill begins again.

5. Player X3 must not allow 3 to drive to the inside (our 1-2-2 zone rule—you should use yours).

6. If 3 shoots, X3 and 3 battle for the rebound. After 3 scores or X3 gets the rebound, the players rotate.

7. Your coach can shoot anytime he wishes. This makes X3, 5, and 3 battle for the rebound. It is X3's responsibility to rebound the weak side (block out 5).

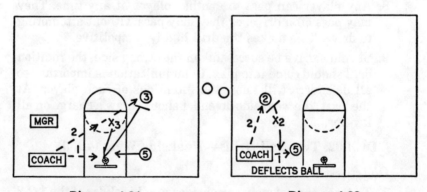

Diagram 4-21   Diagram 4-22

Drill 83: Two-Ball Drills—Strongside Wing (4, 5)

Objectives:

1. To teach the defensive wing man his slides in the 1-2-2 zone (can be used to teach guards of the 2-1-2 and wing men of the 1-3-1).
2. To teach your defensive wing man to help inside yet recover to his own man.
3. To teach hustling zone defense.
4. To condition defensively.
5. To teach one-on-one offensive and defensive play.
6. To teach defensive rebounding.
7. To teach the dive drill.

Procedure:

1. Line up players as shown in Diagram 4-22.
2. Rotate from 2 to X2 to 5 to end of the line. First player in line becomes the new 2.
3. A coach passes back and forth with 2 while X2 reacts as he would in the slides of the 1-2-2 zone. When the coach wants, he passes inside to 5; X2 must deflect this pass.
4. Coach picks the second ball up off the floor and passes quickly to 2. Player 2 goes one-on-one against X2. Give 2 two dribbles to score or he must pass back to the coach. Defender X2 must not allow 2 to drive inside (our 1-2-2 zone rule—you use yours). Player 5 retrieves the deflected ball and lays it at the coach's feet while 2 and X2 are going one-on-one; 5 returns to his position at low post.
5. The drill continues until 2 shoots. Then the group rotates.
6. Coach can shoot requiring X2 to box-out 2 and get the rebound.

Drill 84: Strotum Drill (4B, 5)

Objectives:

1. To teach two baseline defenders (X4 and X5 in Diagram 4-23) to act in unison while playing a zone defense (1-2-2).
2. To teach two baseline defenders their responsibilities in a 1-2-2 match-up zone defense.

3. To teach inside defenders to cover the low-post positions.

4. To teach defenders how to cover the corner positions yet be able to control the low big blocks.

5. To teach 1 and 2 to pass inside to the post.

6. To teach 4 and 5 proper methods of posting up.

7. To teach hustling defense; good for defensive conditioning.

Procedure:

1. Line up players as shown in Diagram 4-23.

2. Rotate each side from corner player to post man to defensive post man to end of the line. Player who is first in each line becomes the new corner player: from 1 to 5 to X5 to end of the line; from 2 to 4 to X4 to end of the line.

3. Coach passes to either 1 or to 2 (1 in Diagram 4-23).

4. Players X4 and X5 react together. Player X5 in Diagram 4-23 goes out to get 1; 1 may drive or shoot or pass inside to 5. Defender X4 comes over to cover 5 as the pass was in the air to 1; X5 must get to the corner as 1 receives the ball. This prevents the jump shot and it prevents the fake drive. Player 5, meanwhile, tries to post up X4.

5. If nothing becomes available to 1 or to 5, 1 passes back to the coach. Players X4 and X5 react back to their defensive low-post duties. You can, if you like, permit 4 and 5 to try to post up and receive a pass from the coach.

6. Your coach can continue the drill by passing back to 1 or reversing the ball around to 2. If the ball goes to 2, X4 hustles out to the corner to cover 2 and X5 races over to cover 4. If nothing becomes available, 2 passes back to the coach and the drill continues.

Drill 85: Two-Ball Drills—Baseline (4B, 5)

Objectives:

1. To teach inside defenders of the 1-2-2 zone how to defend the low post yet cover their corner responsibilities.

2. To teach hustling zone defense.

3. To teach defensive conditioning.

4. To teach one-on-one defense and offense.

5. To teach defensive rebounding.

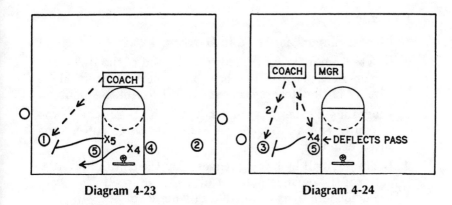

Diagram 4-23   Diagram 4-24

Procedure:

1. Line up players as shown in Diagram 4-24.

2. Rotate from 3 to X4 to 5 to end of the line. First player in line becomes the new 3; 3 and the coach pass the ball back and forth to begin the drill.

3. Coach finally passes inside to 5. Defender X4 must deflect this pass. Coach immediately picks extra ball up off the floor and passes to 3; X4 must hurry out to cover 3. Player 5 retrieves the deflected pass and passes to the manager who puts the ball at the coach's feet.

4. Player 3 goes one-on-one against X4; X4 must not let 3 drive the baseline.

5. You should limit 3 to two dribbles. If 3 cannot get a good shot in two dribbles, he passes to the coach. Coach passes to 5; X4 must deflect this pass. Coach picks up the other ball and passes to 3; X4 hurries out to defend against 3, and the drill continues.

6. Coach can shoot, requiring X4 to box out 5 for the rebound.

7. Coach can make the drill competitive by requiring that 3 or 5 replace X4 when X4 stops their one-on-one move.

Drill 86: Back-Men Head-Turning Drill (4B, 5)

Objectives:

1. To teach the "back" defenders of a zone to always know where potential cutters are.

2. To teach defenders to play on the plane of greatest peripheral view.

3. To teach one-on-one offense and defense while playing a zone.

Procedure:

1. Line up players as shown in Diagram 4-25.
2. Rotate from offense to defense to the end of the line. First players in each of the lines become the new attackers. Make sure all back defensive candidates get to run the drill.
3. Diagram 4-25 shows two defenders of the 1-2-2 zone. If you intend to run a 2-3 zone you could use three cutters and three defenders.
4. Begin the drill by having players cut. Coach can hit either cutter if the defenders do not play the cuts well. You want the defenders to execute rules of your zone.
5. Begin the drill by not allowing the receivers to shoot. When they receive a pass, they fake, then pass back out to the coach. After the defenders begin to understand coverage, you can allow the receivers to work their offensive moves and try to score.

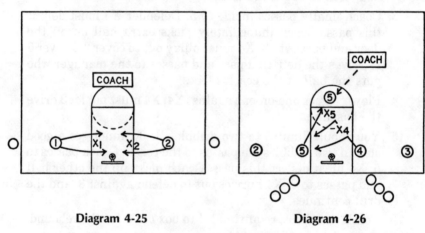

Diagram 4-25   Diagram 4-26

Drill 87: Scissors (4B, 5)

Objectives:

1. To teach the inside defenders the defensive scissors move. When we play a 1-2-2 zone our inside men stay with the flash pivots. The other low-post defender then runs the baseline as in a 1-3-1 zone. This requires X4 to cover a low post who moves from one side of the court to the other—a scissors move.
2. To teach defense of the low-post attackers.
3. To teach defense of the hi-lo offensive attack.

4. To teach one-on-one offense and defense inside.
5. To teach the lob-pass defender to move back into the potential receiver in the lane.

Procedure:

1. Line up players as shown in Diagram 4-26.
2. Rotate from offense to defense to the end of the line. First two players in line become the new inside attackers, 4 and 5.
3. Coach stands out front and allows 4 and 5 to flash pivot. When coach wants, he passes to the flash-pivot attacker (5 in Diagram 4-26). The other attacker immediately rolls across the lane, and 4 and 5 play a hi-lo two-on-two inside game.
4. You can alter the drill by putting in players 2 and 3. When 2 and 3 are inserted, you add the Strotum Drill (Drill 84) to the Scissors drill. These two drills allow continuous drilling of the post coverages in the basic 1-2-2 and in the 1-2-2 match-up zone defense.
5. Player 5 can pass back out to the coach. Do not allow a forced pass or a bad shot.

Drill 88: Back-Men Movement Drill (4B, 5)

Objectives:

1. To teach the back two defenders (X5 and X4) of the 1-3-1, the 1-2-2, or the match-up zone their slides as they follow the passing of the ball.
2. To teach one-on-one defense and offense while operating under zone conditions.
3. To teach passing against a zone.
4. To teach the scissoring movements of the match-up zone.

Procedure:

1. Line up five attackers as shown in Diagram 4-27.
2. Make sure all candidates for the X5 and X4 positions get to play those positions.
3. Begin the drill by allowing only passing to the next man. When you feel your defenders can make their slides quickly and accurately, you can allow skip passing.

4. Begin the drill by not allowing shooting. When the defenders have mastered the slides (your sliding rules), allow 3, 4, and 5 to shoot or drive when open.

5. As 1 passes to 3, X4 slides out to the corner to cover 3. If 3 drives baseline, X5 and X4 trap 3. Player X5, upon seeing the pass go to 3, slides down and covers the big block. When 3 passes back out to 1, X5 slides back to high post and X4 covers strongside low post. If 1 passes to 5, X5 and X4 play tandem defense. If 1 passes to 2 or if 5 passes to 2, X5 drops to low post on the strong side and X4 comes up to cover a pass into 5. Or, if you are scissoring, X5 would stay at high post and X4 would run the baseline as in the 1-3-1 zone. The pass from 2 to 4 would have X5 in the corner and X4 at the low big block unless scissoring was in effect. If the two defenders had called "scissors," X4 would cover 4 in the corner and X5 would cover the low-post big block.

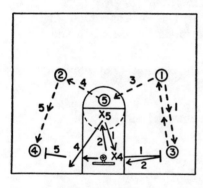

Diagram 4-27

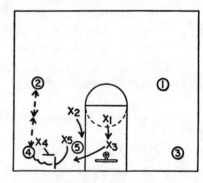

Diagram 4-28

Drill 89: Baseline-Trap-and-Dive Drill (3, 4, 5)

Objectives:

1. To teach the slides of the 1-2-2 zone.

2. To teach the proper defenders to dive on the inside passes to 5.

3. To teach the proper trapping techniques when a defensive breakdown occurs and allows the baseline drive: Defenders X5 and X4 trap; X3 covers pass to center; and X1 drops to defend the basket area.

4. To teach helping on lob passes inside.

5. To teach closing the gap.

6. To teach the rotation drill.

Procedure:

1. Line up five attackers and five defenders as shown in Diagram 4-28.

2. Rotate so that each defender will get to play the area of the 1-2-2 zone he will be responsible for.

3. Players 1 and 3 may not move when the ball is on the side of 2 and 4. Players 2 and 4 may not move when the ball is on the side of 1 and 3.

4. Players 2 and 4 pass the ball back and forth until they can get it inside to 5. If, after a few passes they cannot get the ball into 5, they may reverse the ball to the side of the court where 1 and 3 are located. If a pass goes inside to 5, the proper defender (X2 or X4) must dive and force the ball back out.

5. Players 2 or 4 may drive any time they have the ball. This requires proper closing-the-gap techniques. Should the driver penetrate beyond where you can close the gap, the rotation drill should begin.

6. Should 2 drive to the inside, X1 and X2 trap 2 (our rule). Should 2 drive outside, X4 closes the gap (our rule). Should 4 drive inside, X2 closes the gap. Should 4 drive baseline, X5 and X4 trap (also our rule). X3 comes over to cover the center and X1 drops to cover the basket area. X2 covers the middle lane. This forces the ball back out, and it frequently results in a turnover.

7. Whenever 2 and 4 want, they may reverse the ball to 1. Player 5 immediately goes to the low-post area on the side of the court where 1 and 3 are located. Player 5 immediately tries to post up big; and the drill continues.

Drill 90: 1-3-1 Zone Breakdown Drill (4C, 5)

Objectives:

1. To teach the duties and slides of the zone of your choice (1-3-1 in Diagram 4-29).

2. To teach correct passing techniques.

3. To teach hustling defense from a zone.

Procedure:

1. Line up players as shown in Diagram 4-29.

2. Make sure all candidates for X1, X5, and X2 get to play those defensive positions. Put the remainder of your squad in the numbered slots, filling as many as the number of players in your squad permits.

3. As the attackers pass the ball, have them hold the ball for a two count before passing again. Check to see if the slides are made accurately.

4. You can use a different number of combinations of defenders: you could use only the wings, X3 and X4; or you could use only the point and the baseline defenders, X1 and X2; or you could use all perimeter defenders, X1, X2, X3, and X4; or you could use the entire team.

5. When you use the entire team, allow the attackers to pass the ball as quickly as they can. Allow the attackers to shoot if possible. Your defense should be able to contest any shot if they hustle and play good team defense. Do not allow any cutting. The numbered positions represent spots where cutting would naturally occur.

6. Diagram 4-29 shows the point, post, and baseline defenders of the 1-3-1, but you can use another zone and break it down in a similar manner.

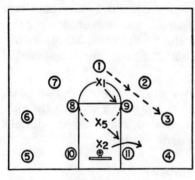

Diagram 4-29

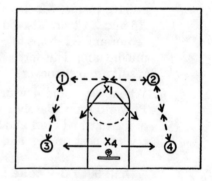

Diagram 4-30

Drill 91: 1-3-1 Zone Drill: Point and Baseline (4C, 5)

Objectives:

1. To teach X1 and X4 to cover their positions instinctively.

2. To teach X1 to lane.

3. To teach X4 to fight over low-post screens.

4. To teach lob passes.

5. To teach players to shoot as they receive the pass. This requires proper footwork.

Procedure:

1. Line up players as shown in Diagram 4-30.

2. Be sure each potential point and baseline man gets to work at those positions.

3. No diagonal passes allowed. Attackers must pass the ball around the horn.

4. Only corner men can shoot.

5. Defender X1 must make 1 and 2 lob ball if X4 is to have a chance to cover both corners. X1, in other words, must lane the pass between 1 and 2.

6. Players may not dribble or move.

7. You can put two screeners on the big blocks to alter the drill. By placing two screeners on the big blocks, X4 must avoid the screens in going from corner to corner. You could also add on X5, the center in the 1-3-1 zone. Now the screens on the big blocks can post up. Also, the corner man could drive and X4 and X5 would activate the Trapping drill (Drill 65).

Drill 92: 1-3-1 Zone Defense: Wing Drill (4C, 5)

Objectives:

1. To teach proper defensive wing coverage from 1-3-1 and 1-2-2 zone defenses.

2. To teach the guards to shoot quickly and accurately.

3. To teach crosscourt skip passing (not an offensive sin).

4. To teach defensive rebounding while playing a 1-3-1 or 1-2-2 zone defense.

Procedure:

1. Line up players as shown in Diagram 4-31.

2. Be sure all potential wing men get to run these positions.

3. Players 1 and 2 may throw lob passes. Any player may pass crosscourt except 3 and 4 cannot pass to each other; however, 3 and 4 may pass to any other player.

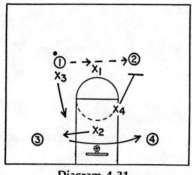

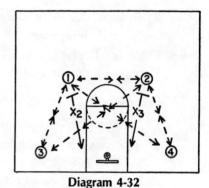

| Diagram 4-31 | Diagram 4-32 |

4. Only the guards, 1 and 2, may shoot. If 3 or 4 should receive a crosscourt pass, they may shoot the lay-up.

5. Defenders X2 and X3 must learn their proper positioning with respect to the ball; they must intercept passes thrown crosscourt; they must block out on any shot attempt.

6. Players 1 and 2 may not dribble or move.

Drill 93: 1-3-1 Zone: Point, Baseline, and Wings (4C, 5)

Objectives:

1. To drill your point, wings, and baseline defenders on the proper slides of the 1-3-1 zone.

2. To teach closing the gap.

3. To teach rotation.

4. To teach passing against a zone.

Procedure:

1. Put four attackers in the four open perimeter slots of the 1-3-1 zone defense (Diagram 4-32). You may put 3 and 4 in the corner or on the big blocks.

2. Players 1, 2, 3, and 4 pass the ball until one of them gets a drive or a jump shot. Defenders X1, X2, X3, and X4 must cover their areas without allowing the drive or the jumper.

3. You can allow X1, X2, X3 and X4 to trap if that is part of your team defense.

4. Offensive players may not dribble or move. After defenders have improved to the point where they can consistently stop the jump shot, you may want to add driving. This enables your defenders to work on closing the gap and rotation. But these drives should come immediately after the driver has received a pass.

5

Match-Up Zone Defensive Drills

Match-up zones are increasing in popularity with every passing season, but many coaches still are not sure they can teach the match-up effectively. Many coaches get disenchanted when they teach the match-up zone only because their initial conception of the match-up was inaccurate. They believed, erroneously, in the beginning, that the match-up was the answer to all their defensive problems. There is *no* single answer to all defensive problems. The match-up is not a panacea to correct all things. But the match-up is a most powerful defensive tool. It is not an answer to everything; but it is an answer to many offensive attacks.

The coach who tries the match-up and becomes disillusioned figures he does not know enough about it or he is teaching it wrong. Neither is probably the truth.

Match-ups can be taught by drills just like all the other defenses and just as thoroughly and easily. All the drills marked with the Number 5 can be used to make your match-up that much more effective. You choose the drills you want as your primary teaching tools. Then add the other drills as auxillary drills to supplement your teaching.

First, you should choose your starting zone defense because that would eliminate the two other zone sets of drills (4A for 2-1-2, 4B for 1-2-2, and 4C for 1-3-1. Then you should include all the drills in this chapter. Finally, you must consider all the other drills marked with the Number 5.

Drill 94: Baseline Tandem Drill (4B, 4C, 5, 7, 8, and 9)

Objectives:

1. To teach the tandem slides of the match-up zone defense.
2. To teach the slides of the 1-2-2 and the 1-3-1 zone defenses.

3. To teach tandem defense against fast breaks.

4. To teach how to stop the breakaway basket when your man-to-man and zone presses are broken.

5. To teach hustling zone defense.

6. To develop reaction as the ball is being passed.

7. To teach perimeter passing.

Procedure:

1. Line up players as shown in Diagram 5-1.

2. Make sure all players get to play both the front and the back positions of the defense. One proper rotation would be for 5 to go to 4 to 3 to X5 to X4 to the end of the line. First player in line becomes the next 5.

3. Players 3, 4, and 5 pass around the perimeter. They may even throw skip passes.

4. There is always one defender on the ball and one defender protecting the basket area. Player X5 guards 5 and X4 protects the basket before the first pass. Once 5 passes, X4 goes to the player receiving the pass and X5 drops back to cover the basket (pass is from 5 to 4 in Diagram 5-1). When 4 passes, X5 will go to cover the receiver and X4 will drop back to the basket. The drill continues in this manner for fifteen seconds, then rotates.

5. Begin by not allowing any shots. After the players have learned their slides and perform them instinctively, you can allow shots and drives. No attacker should ever drive all the way to the basket without charging if the defender under the basket is alert and does his job.

6. Lastly, put the attackers in three lines at midcourt and have them perform a live three-on-two fast break.

Drill 95: Match-Up "Scissors" Drill (4B, 5)

Objectives:

1. To teach inside defenders of the match-up zone defense how they can cover the inside post play.

2. To teach "scissoring."

3. To teach defense of the hi-lo offensive game.

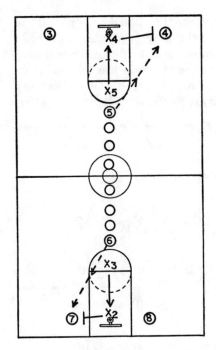

Diagram 5-1

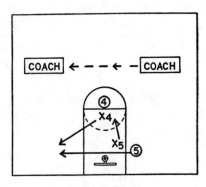

Diagram 5-2

Procedure:

1. Line up players as shown in Diagram 5-2. Make sure all candidates for X4 and X5 get to play those positions.

2. Two coaches pass the ball outside; 5 breaks along the baseline. As the ball is passed between the two coaches X4 and X5 can exchange post players or they can "scissor" (stay with the player they are defending).

3. After learning this slide, you can allow X5 to call "scissor." This means X4 and X5 will exchange coverage sides of the court because X5 has now told X4 he is going with 5 to the side normally covered by X4. Defender X5 would stay with the cutting 5 and X4 would stay at high post on 4.

4. You can combine "scissors" with the regular slide by going to Diagram 5-3. When your coach passes the ball back to the original passer, X4 drops to cover low post and X5 becomes the new high-post defender (Diagram 5-3). Of course, X5 could have yelled "scissors" again which would have left X4 at high post and X5 running the baseline.

5. Coaches can pass inside anytime they find 4 or 5 open. If the coach should hit high post, the players would run a hi-lo option and the defenders must stop it. If coach hits a low-post attacker, they go one-on-one while the high-post attacker breaks low for a pass or a rebound. Don't allow any forced shots. Attackers can always pass back to the coaches.

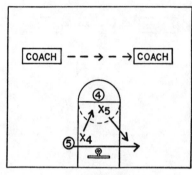

Diagram 5-3

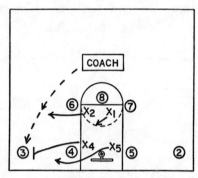

Diagram 5-4

Drill 96: Strotum Drill with Two Guards (5)

Objectives:

1. To teach coverage of the baseline by X4 and X5.
2. To teach guards (or wings) to cover high post when ball is in the corner.
3. To teach slides of the match-up zone.
4. To teach posting up offensively and to teach your defense about the post-up maneuvers.
5. To teach closing the gap and rotations.
6. To teach trapping of the baseline drive.

Procedure:

1. Line players up as shown in Diagram 5-4. Make sure everyone who is to play defensive perimeter plays the X1 and X2 positions and everyone who is to defend on the baseline plays X4 and X5 positions.
2. Players X4 and X5 defend the baseline as in the Strotum Drill (Drill 84).
3. With the ball in the corner (Diagram 5-4), X2 covers the pass into the high-post player number 6 and X1 covers the

pass into high-post player number 8. If ball is passed to 2's corner, X1 would not allow a pass into player number 7 and X2 would keep pass from player number 8.

4. With ball in the corner, 3 may pass only to 4, 8, or 6. Player 3 can drive baseline, dive inside, or shoot. If 3 drives the baseline, X4 and X5 execute the Trapping drill (Drill 65). If 3 drives inside, X2 must Close the Gap (Drill 38). If 3 escapes the trap or drives by the closing-the-gap maneuver, the Rotation drill is activated (Drill 55). If nothing develops, 3 passes back to the coach. Coach can only pass to 2, 3, 4, or 5.

Drill 97: The Nine-Man Drill (4B, 5)

Objectives:

1. To teach all defenders except point players their slides in the match-up zone or their slides of the 1-2-2 zone.
2. To teach box-out techniques when a shot is taken against the match-up or 1-2-2 zone.
3. To teach closing the gap, rotation, and trapping along the baseline.
4. To teach hustling match-up zone defense (*or* get a hand in the shooter's face).

Procedure:

1. Line up players as shown in Diagram 5-5.
2. Be sure all players who are candidates for X2, X3, X4, and X5 get to play those positions.
3. Begin the drill with 1 having the basketball. Player 1 passes to 2 and the match-up defenders react: Player X3 picks up 2, X2 sags to pick up 3, X5 and X4 change men or scissor (see Drill 87 and Drill 95).
4. If 2 should pass to 4, X5 would match up on 4. Defender X4 would cover the low post.
5. At first, just allow passing. After defenders learn the slides of their match-up zone, then you can begin allowing shots. Later, you can put in cutting (Drills 70, 71, and 103).
6. Have defenders use correct box-out techniques on any shot attempt.
7. On any pass into pivot, defenders guarding 3 and 4 must cover their cuts to the basket man-to-man.

8. Later, you may allow driving as well as shooting. When drives begin, the proper defender must close the gap, rotate, or trap along the baseline.

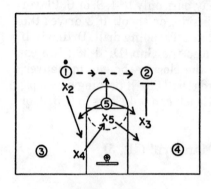
Diagram 5-5

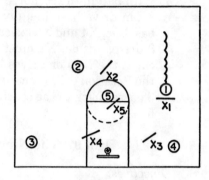
Diagram 5-6

Drill 98: Match-Up Coverage Drill (5)

Objectives:

1. To teach your match-up coverage rule.
2. To teach proper weakside sag.
3. To teach zone defenders how to use the interception stance.
4. To teach defenders the proper body position so they will always be on the plane of greatest peripheral view.

Procedure:

1. Line up players as shown in Diagram 5-6.
2. Let the five attackers come downcourt and set up in any formation (including overloads) that you desire.
3. See if the defenders know your match-up coverage rule: Let X1 take 1 on one trip, and X1 may take 2 on the next trip— all other defenders match up from whomever X1 takes. In Diagram 5-6, X1 takes 1.
4. Defender X2 must sag in the passing lane into 5; he should be in his interception stance if you are laning. X2 can cut off the drive by 1 into the middle; His body must be such that he can peripherally see 1, 2, and 3.
5. Defender X3 positions himself so he can see almost all of the court, using his interception stance if you are laning. If

you are containing, X3 should see all five attackers, and he should be two steps toward the basket and one step from his man.

6. Defender X4 would cover 3 according to the match-up rules. X4 must play on the plane of greatest peripheral view: He must see all of the court. X4 can probably locate four steps toward the basket and two steps from his man. From this positioning, he can protect the middle and he can accept strongside cutters.

7. Defender X5 can play to the side of 5, preventing 5 from getting the ball. If he prefers, X5 can play behind 5, trusting X2 to discourage the inside pass. You, as the defensive coach, can decide. But, in either case, X5 should make himself big, arms up or to the side, making 1 think the inside passing lane to any cutter is closed.

Drill 99: Three-on-Four Clearout Drill (5)

Objectives:

1. To teach defenders proper sag as ball is being passed.
2. To teach defenders to go with the cutters to the ballside free throw-lane line before releasing their cutters to a weakside man.
3. To teach closing the gap.
4. To teach defenders how to cover one-on-one on the perimeter.
5. To teach defenders away from the ball the interceptor's stance, using proper peripheral view.
6. To teach match-up zone defenders not to allow a side of the court to be cleared.

Procedure:

1. Line up three offensive players against three defenders. Defender X4 begins as the weakside helper (Diagram 5-7).
2. Rotate from 1 to X1 to 2 to X2 to 3 to X3 to X4 to end of the line. First man in line becomes the new 1.
3. Attackers pass the ball around until one of them decides to go one-on-one. You can use a signal to tell which player to go one-on-one.
4. The defenders on clearout cutters follow them at least to the

free throw line on the ballside where he is released to the weakside deep defender (X3 or X4). The defender on the cutter then returns to his area or man to cover.

5. Diagram 5-7 shows 3 clearing out. But 1 could pass to 3 and 1 clears out; X4 would pick up either cutter.

6. On cuts through the zone a pass can be attempted. There is no center so the attacker cannot stop in the lane nor can he post up, but he can cut through the lane.

7. The man with the ball can go one-on-one anytime he wishes.

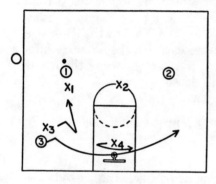   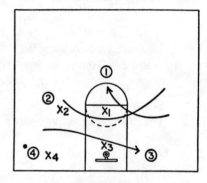

Diagram 5-7   Diagram 5-8

Drill 100: Four Men on the Perimeter Cutting Drill (5)

Objectives:

1. To teach defending the cutter.
2. To teach the cutter rule.
3. To teach sagging the three-step drill.
4. To teach playing on the plane of greatest peripheral view.
5. To teach proper coverage of perimeter men with the ball in the corner.

Procedure:

1. Line up four attackers against four defenders (Diagram 5-8).
2. Let the ball be passed into the corners.
3. Have the four outside offensive players cut through the lane in an assortment of ways. Have defenders execute their proper shifts. After each player cuts through the key area, he moves back to the perimeter.

4. Check to see if X3, X2, or X4, whichever is weakside deep defender, has counted and is defending the fourth perimeter man from the corner.

Drill 101: Coverage-Rule Drill (5)

Objectives:

1. To teach closing the gap.
2. To teach the coverage rule.
3. To teach the three-step drill.
4. To teach defenders to respond to the next offense you will face.
5. To teach playing on the plane of greatest peripheral view.

Procedure:

1. Allow five offensive players to bring the ball downcourt while the defense sets in a standard 1-3-1 zone (or the zone of your choice) (Diagram 5-9).
2. Start by requiring that the offense line up in a typical or basic set used against the 1-3-1. Check to see if the matchups are correct according to who has whom and positioning (three-step drill and the plane of greatest peripheral view).
3. You may then allow passing with no offensive player movement.
4. You can advance to allowing drives and forcing defenders to close the gap, but do not allow man movement.
5. Allow cutters after you teach the cutter's rule (See Drill 102).
6. Repeat the first four steps by having the attackers start in an overload alignment.
7. Repeat the first four steps by having the attackers start in any free-lance array they wish.
8. Repeat the first four steps by having the attackers use the formations of your next opponent.

Drill 102: Match-Up Cutter's-Rule Drill (5)

Objectives:

1. To teach coverage of the cutters.

2. To teach accepting and releasing cutters.

3. To teach the cutter's rule.

4. To teach closing the gaps (by letting players drive while cutters cut).

5. To teach body checking.

6. To teach sagging the three-step drill.

7. To teach the interception stance (X3 could be in an interception stance in Diagram 5-10).

8. To teach playing on the plane of greatest peripheral view.

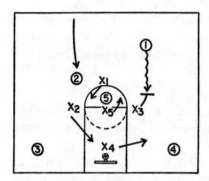 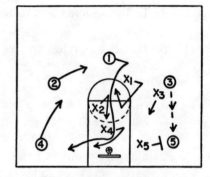

Diagram 5-9   Diagram 5-10

Procedure:

1. Line up five attackers and five defenders as shown in Diagram 5-10.

2. You can switch from five, to four, to three perimeter players as you feel the need to drill. Here we will describe a five-man perimeter situation.

3. Coach numbers offensive positions and calls out the numbers when he wants a cutter. That cutter can be ordered to cut to the baseline or wherever you want him. Or the cutter can decide for himself.

4. The other offensive players fill in the holes, keeping the continuity alive.

5. Diagram 5-10, for example, shows our weakside coverage of cutters. If you go back and use the other drills in this chapter, you will notice the coverage is consistent. Whichever part of your cutter defense is weak, work on that part in this drill. You can also allow your cutters to cut freely,

especially after you have taught them your complete defense. In this diagram, you will want X1 to come one step below the free throw line where he will hear X4 call "release." X4 keeps 1; X2, meanwhile, rotated down onto 4. Defender X1 would pick up 2.

6. Players 2 and 4, for example, could exchange places. 2 could flash to the strongside while 4 rolls to fill 2's vacant spot. If 2 does not get the ball, 2 would fill 4's vacant spot. You could let 3 cut and 1, 2, and 4 fill one position over. This would teach strongside wing coverage.

7. Proper fundamentals of releasing and accepting cutters must be observed and corrected.

Drill 103: Accepting-Cutter Drill (5)

Objectives:

1. To teach your coverage rules on cutters.
2. To teach sagging in and toward each pass (after all, you are in a zone).
3. To teach accepting and releasing cutters.
4. To teach adjusting with each pass.
5. To teach playing on the plane of greatest peripheral view.
6. To teach trapping along the baseline, closing the gap, and rotation.

Procedure:

1. Line up four perimeter attackers and drill on coverage on the outside (Diagram 5-11).
2. Make sure each candidate for X1, X2, X3, and X4 get to drill at their positions.
3. Defenders X2, X1, and X3 move a step toward the pass and two steps toward the basket while the ball is in the air from 2 to 4.
4. Player X3, the weakside deep defender, sliding back to the area of the free throw line on the ball-side, plays on the plane of greatest peripheral view. He does this so he can see the entire court.
5. Defender X2 is in an interceptor's stance. Defender X3 picks up cutter 2 as 2 cuts into the lane; X3 also knows he must mentally play in the lane between 3 and 4. Defensive

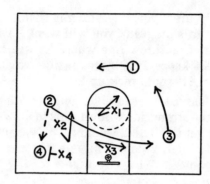

Diagram 5-11

player X3 knows that the quicker he picks up 2, the quicker X2 can slide back out on 1 who has rotated to 2's old spot. The offense must rotate a player to that spot, or 4 will not have anyone to receive a pass if 4 gets into trouble.

6. When X3 feels he has 2 covered, he says "release." This cues X2 to hurry mentally back into position on 1. If 1 can get the shot off before X2 physically arrives, we want him to shoot. If 1 cannot, we want 1 to pass to 4 and cut through with each offender rotating one more position. This continues until X2 and X3 learn to release and accept cutters.

7. The drill may be run from any cutting position on the court. You may allow any passer to cut. Then you may allow even nonpassers to cut. This allows the offense continuous movement.

8. After defensing the cutter has been mastered, you can allow the attacker with the ball to drive. Whenever that attacker drives, the defender nearest the driver should close the gap. If the gap closing defender arrives too late, then the deep defender activates the rotation drill. And if the drive occurs along the baseline, your two baseline defenders should run your trapping drill.

6

Half-Court Pressure Zone Defensive Drills

Defensive half-court zone traps can present unbelievable problems to attacking teams. But built into those problems are also defensive vulnerabilities: Double-teamers and gap shooters operate so near their defensive basket that easy buckets can be scored unless proper team recovery techniques are drilled upon until mastered. The drills in this chapter offer the coach who is considering using a half-court zone trap many opportunities to correct those defensive vulnerabilities.

Fundamental trapping drills as well as team drills teaching the team trap of your choice are offered. These drills should be adapted by the wise coach to teach the slides of the actual trap under consideration. Constant drilling will make these slides automatic and instinctive, greatly increasing the quickness of execution, a component visible in all championship squads.

Drill 104: Two vs. Three Continuous Trap (4B, 4C, 6, 7, 8)

Objectives:

1. Half-court traps require weakside wings to cover inside passing lanes yet recover to trapping responsibilities when on the strong side (ball-side). This drill will teach the wings, X2 and X3, to react instinctively to these two responsibilities.

2. To teach correct trapping techniques.

3. To teach laning (by X1) to slow down offensive quick passing.

4. To teach proper angles of interception.

5. To teach anticipation and proper body positioning.

109

Procedure:

1. Line up players as shown in Diagram 6-1.
2. Rotate from 1 to X1 to X2 to X3 to 2 to 5 to the end of the line.
3. Coach begins drill by passing to either 1 or 2.
4. Either player 1 or 2 immediately tries to attack by dribbling or by passing inside to 5. The two players without the ball (2 and 5 in Diagram 6-1) cannot move until they receive the ball.
5. Players 1 and 2 can drive at anytime when they have the ball.
6. Any pass inside to 5 activates 5's drive to the basket. The defensive wing who is responsible for the inside pass must contain 5's drive. If 5 cannot score in two dribbles, he passes back outside and the drill continues.
7. You can not allow any of the attackers to move by dribbling. By allowing only passing, you can have a continuous trapping and shooting-the-gap drill.

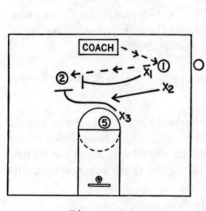

Diagram 6-1

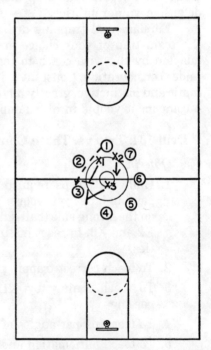

Diagram 6-2

Drill 105: Bull-in-Ring Trap Drill (6, 7, 8)

Objectives:

1. To teach your trapping techniques and rules.
2. To teach a defender to shoot the gap.
3. To teach passing under extreme pressure.
4. To teach careful passing and stepping toward the pass to receive it.
5. To teach fake passing, much needed for attacking zone defenses.
6. To teach good defensive judgment.

Procedures:

1. Line up players as shown in Diagram 6-2.
2. Whenever X1, X2, or X3 deflect a pass, they take the place of the passer. The passer and the other two defenders stay on defense.
3. A passer may not pass to the men next to him. A passer may pass to anyone else.
4. Be sure when there is a completed pass that your defenders rotate according to the rules of your presses (our rule— container rotates, trapper stays).
5. In Diagram 6-2, X1 and X2 trap 1. Player X3 tries to steal or deflect 1's pass. Player 1's pass to 3, when completed, would show X3 and X1 trapping 3; X2 would then become the gap shooter, trying to steal or deflect any pass 3 would make. Defender X2 wants to use good judgment.

Drill 106: Two-on-Two Trapping Drills (6, 7, 8, 9)

Objectives:

1. To teach two defenders to trap a dribbler who has already begun his drive.
2. If you include X3 in the drill, you use X3 as a gap shooter. Under that condition, your drill would also teach gap shooting.
3. To teach X1 and X2 quick reactions to a specified offensive maneuver.
4. To learn how to cover throwback passes.

Procedures:

1. Line up players as shown in Diagram 6-3.
2. Rotate from 1 to 2 to X1 to X2 to X3 (if he is in the drill) to the end of the line. First player in line becomes the next 1.
3. Coach can pass to either 1 or 2 to begin the drill. Whoever receives the pass begins his dribble immediately. You can require 1 and 2 to receive the pass in certain spots on the floor.
4. Players X1 and X2 begin immediately to approach the dribbling 1, trying to bring 1 under control and trap him.
5. You should also alter from day to day where X1 and X2 are to begin their traps. Some days they should trap just over the midcourt line, some days at the end line, and some days at the 28-foot marker.
6. You can enter X3 into the drill and allow him to shoot the gap for interceptions. Should the throwback pass to 2 be completed, you can run the Throwback Pass drill (Drill 138).
7. You can allow a two-on-two fast break if any steals result from the double-team pressure (three-on-two if you have included an X3 in the drill).

Drill 107: Two-on-Three Half-Court Trap Drill (6, 7, 8, 9)

Objectives:

1. To teach continuous trapping and shooting the gap.
2. To teach attackers to handle the ball under extreme pressure.
3. To teach players away from the ball to free themselves for a pass.
4. To teach proper team rotations out of traps.

Procedure:

1. Line up players as shown in Diagram 6-4.
2. After going through the drill two or three times, have the defenders and the attackers rotate to the opposite lines. Make sure you begin with the defensive line much longer than the offensive line.
3. Players 1 and 2 are to attack X1, X2, and X3.

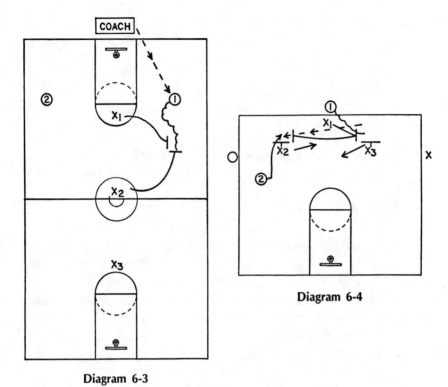

Diagram 6-4

Diagram 6-3

4. In Diagram 6-4, X1 and X3 trap 1. Defender X2 denies 2 the ball. When 2 frees himself, X2 contains 2 until X1 arrives to help trap; X3 keeps 1 from the ball, using denial tactics.

5. You need a team rule when playing man-to-man which will tell the defenders who is to trap and who is to shoot the gap (our rule—trapper stays, container rotates; if playing a zone, you simply run your slides; there is more structure when playing a zone).

6. If 1 and 2 score, you rotate the next group on the floor, or you can rotate the next group after 1 and 2 have scored twice.

7. If X1, X2, and X3 steal a pass or rebound a missed shot, X1, X2, and X3 fast break against 1 and 2 (see Drill 148, Tandem Defense into Pressure Defense). You could even continue your drill into a two-on-one fast break back down the floor with 1 and 2 attacking the scorer among X1, X2, and X3 (see Drill 146).

Drill 108: Midcourt Trapping Drill
and Shooting the Gap (6, 7, 8, 9)

Objectives:

1. To teach passing under control.
2. To teach trapping a moving passer or dribbler.
3. To teach shooting the gap.
4. To teach the looping dribble out of a trap.
5. To teach fast-breaking tactics of three versus two.

Procedures:

1. Line up players as shown in Diagram 6-5.
2. Leave the defenders for several attacks, then move three more defenders out, making sure all defenders get to play their positions.
3. Have two offensive players pass the ball until they near midcourt. One of the offensive players then dribbles to split the two defenders.
4. Players X1 and X2, the two defenders on the side of the ball, trap the dribbler; X3 shoots the gap.
5. You can extend the drill by having three offensive players run a passing figure-eight weave. Under these conditions, X3, the gap shooter, would have two potential receivers to cover. He must learn to split these attackers and "to read" the passer.
6. You can allow the drill to be a continuous three-defenders-vs.-two-attackers drill all over the front court until the attackers score or the defenders steal the pass.
7. You can even extend this drill to a three-on-four or a four-on-five drill.
8. Once a score has been made or a steal or defensive rebound results, you can allow the original three defenders to attack the two original attackers in a three-on-two fast break. This allows the original two attackers to play a tandem defense.

Drill 109: Four-on-Two Trap Drill (6, 7, 8, 9)

Objectives:

1. To teach two defenders to trap without allowing the dribbler to escape.

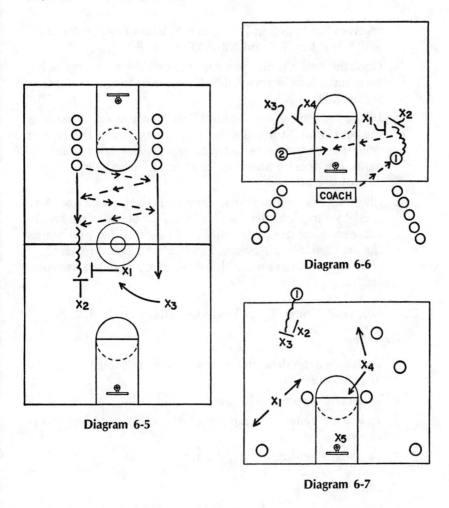

Diagram 6-6

Diagram 6-5

Diagram 6-7

2. To teach a dribbler the methods of escaping a double-team trap.

3. To teach passing out of a trap.

4. To teach attackers to come to meet passes when facing pressure defenses.

Procedures:

1. Line up players as shown in Diagram 6-6.

2. Rotate from 1 and 2 to X1 and X2 to X3 and X4 to the end of the two lines. First player in each line becomes the new 1 and the new 2.

3. Coach begins the drill by passing to either 1 or 2. Whoever

receives the ball, 1 in Diagram 6-6, tries to escape the trap, which is set by X1 and X2 in Diagram 6-6.

4. Once the ball handler picks up his dribble, he passes to his teammate, 2 in Diagram 6-6. Now 2 tries to escape the trap set by X3 and X4.

5. In the beginning you should allow 1 only the right side of the court and 2 the left side. You can also limit the type of dribble each must use to try to escape. But you should advance the drill by allowing freedom of the dribble and freedom of the method.

6. Players 1 and 2 attack until they cross the far baseline. Any steal by any defender results in a four-on-two fast break. After crossing the far baseline, the coach at that end begins the drill back to the original end. After 1 and 2 reach their original starting point, the drill ends, and the rotation occurs.

Drill 110: Half-Court Trap Team-Overload Drill (6, 7, 8, 9)

Objectives:

1. To teach defenders the slides of the half-court trap you intend to use.
2. To teach trapping techniques.
3. To teach defenders to gap potential receivers in their coverage areas.
4. To teach shooting the gap for interceptions.

Procedures:

1. Line up players as shown in Diagram 6-7.
2. Rotate five players from offense to defense. Let the defenders assume some of the spaces of the players who become the next defenders.
3. The proper team members of the half-court trap you are teaching double-team the ball. The others gap the potential pass receivers.
4. If a pass is completed, the two defenders responsible for the trap in that area double-team the new receiver.
5. If a pass is intercepted, allow the defenders to fast break to the opposite end of the court. This may be done with a dummy fast break, or you may designate two attackers to become the tandem defenders once an interception occurs.

7

Full-Court
Man-to-Man
Defensive Drills

Full-court man-to-man defenses should not be as structured as their zone counterparts. Hence, the need for drilling and more drilling.

Spontaneous reactions to offensive maneuvers are the hallmark of well-planned, well-drilled man-to-man presses. Each defender must read how the offense is attacking and each defender must react to what those attacking dictate. This reaction must operate within the principles set forth by the coach for his man-to-man press. Because these offensive situations are so varied, and because any one of these offensive maneuvers may not reoccur often, it is important that each defender know all the team techniques the coach intends to employ for the year. Hence, the need for exclusive drilling.

Exclusive drilling must occur for the run-and-jump techniques, for denial, for face-guarding, for shortstopping, for centerfielding, for leftfielding, for fanning, for funnelling, for trapping and shooting the gap, and for proper recovering. The coach can choose which of the techniques he wants employed. The athletes must be drilled until those chosen by the coach have been mastered to the point of being executed instinctively. All have received more than adequate coverage in this chapter.

Drill 111: Full-Court Approach Drill (6, 7, 8, 9)

Objectives:

1. To condition defensively.
2. To teach drawing the charge, flicking the reverse, stealing

117

the crossover, and turning the attacker three times each half court (see Drill 23, the Full-Court Zigzag Drill).

3. To teach the defender how to approach and bring a hard-driving dribbler under control.

4. To teach offensive dribbling escape maneuvers.

Procedure:

1. Line up players as shown in Diagram 7-1.

2. Rotate the offensive players to the end of the defensive line and the defenders to the end of the offensive line.

3. After running your Full-Court Zigzag drill (Drill 23), begin running this drill.

4. On the first whistle allow the defenders to spring at full speed. When the defenders get near midcourt, blow the whistle to get the dribblers to begin driving at full speed.

5. The defenders must bring the dribblers under control and defense them one-on-one up the court.

6. Defenders must learn to move up fast and still defense the dribbler, bring him under control, and prepare to press again.

7. You begin by not letting the dribblers out of their lane (the three lanes shown in Diagram 7-1). Then you can advance to allowing the dribblers to go anywhere,

8. You could keep the drill under more control by limiting the attackers' moves to only the crossover, or the reverse, or the looping maneuver, or a behind-the-back initial move.

9. The drill ends when the ball has been advanced beyond the far baseline.

Drill 112: Triangle Sliding and Full-Court Press Drill (6, 7, 8, 9)

Objectives:

1. To teach the defensive shuffle slide.

2. To teach sprinting to get defensive position.

3. To teach backpedaling, which gives defenders practice in maintaining body balance.

4. To teach diving on the floor to recover a loose ball.

5. To teach one-on-one full-court offense and defense.

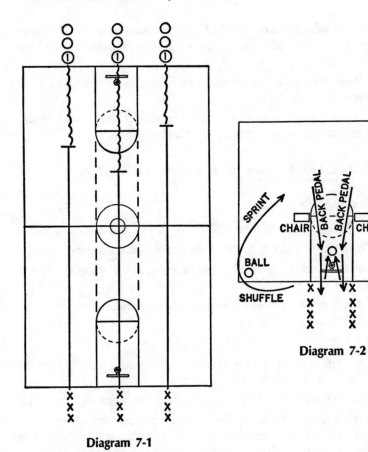

Diagram 7-2

Diagram 7-1

6. To teach conditioning defensively.
7. To teach handling the ball against tremendous defensive pressure.

Procedure:

1. Line up players as shown in Diagram 7-2.
2. On signal, both players slide the baseline facing out of bounds.
3. When defender reaches the corner, he sprints to a point above the chair. Then he backpedals until he crosses the baseline.
4. From the baseline, he dives for the ball (placed in the paint before the drill begins).

5. Player who recovers the ball is on offense. The other player is on defense in a one-on-one Full-Court Zigzag drill (see Drill 23).

6. When players cross opposite baseline, they sprint back to the end of the line.

7. You can speed up the drill by beginning the second group when the first group recovers the loose ball.

Drill 113: Feeling for the Screen Drill (7, 8)

Objectives:

1. To teach defenders to full-court press, yet avoid screens.

2. To teach attackers to drive defenders into screens.

3. To teach drawing the charge, flicking, and forcing change of directions.

4. To teach ball handling under extreme defensive pressure.

Procedure:

1. Line up attackers and defenders in pairs in each lane as shown in Diagram 7-3.

2. Place chairs or football dummies on the floor as screeners.

3. Attackers try to drive their defenders into the chairs. Defenders try to force change of directions, try to draw the charge, or try to flick (if this maneuver is part of your defensive philosophy).

4. Defenders must avoid the chairs as they perform their defensive maneuvers.

5. Attackers go down and back. Then the attackers become defenders and the defenders become attackers. Players 1 and X1 go. When they reach midcourt, 5 and X5 go; 1 and X1 wait at the far baseline until 5 and X5 arrive. Then both groups begin the drill again from the far baseline to the near baseline. Then they rotate from offense to defense.

6. To teach quickness of the feet and better defensive body balance as well as to eliminate that terrible habit of reaching for the ball, you can require that the defenders keep their hands behind their back. An alternative is to require the defenders to hold a towel around their waist.

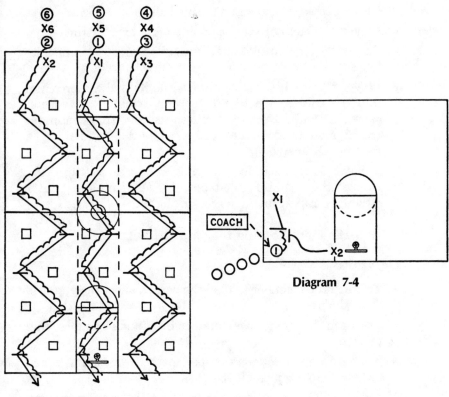

Diagram 7-3

Diagram 7-4

Drill 114: Trapping a Dribbler (6, 7, 8)

Objectives:

1. To teach how to double-team a dribbler correctly.
2. To teach one defender how to contain and another how to double-team. The container is to prevent vertical advancement; the double-teamer is to eliminate the horizontal movement.
3. To teach offensive dribblers to escape the double-team.

Procedure:

1. Line up players as shown in Diagram 7-4.
2. Rotate from 1 to X1 to X2 to the end of the line. First player in line becomes the new 1.

3. Coach passes to 1 to activate the drill.

4. Player 1 tries to break the double-team by dribbling.

5. Player X1 tries to contain 1 until X2 arrives for a double-team.

6. Player 1 keeps his dribble alive while X1 and X2 force him into the corner. We like 1 to keep dribbling because it causes X1 and X2 to force 1 into the corner. This eliminates reaching in to steal the dribble while double-teaming, a cardinal defensive sin.

7. You extend this drill by requiring X1 and X2 to trap 1. If 1 escapes the initial double-team, the defenders must cut 1 off and retrap at another spot on the court.

Drill 115: Shooting-the-Gap Drill (6, 7, 8)

Objectives:

1. To teach the defender to read the passer, shoot the gap, and steal the pass.

2. To teach 1 how to pass and dribble under double-team pressure.

3. To teach double-teamers proper methods of forcing a bad pass to help X3 pick off the pass.

4. To teach X3 perfect position to shoot the gap for a steal.

Procedure:

1. Line up players as shown in Diagram 7-5.

2. Rotate from 1 to X1 to X2 to 3 to 4 to X4 to the end of the line. The first man 1n the line becomes the new 1.

3. Coach passes to 1 to activate the drill.

4. You can begin the drill by not allowing 1 to dribble, or you can begin the drill by letting 1 try to dribble escape X1 and X2 (like in Drill 114).

5. Defenders X1 and X2 double-team 1; X1 and X2 must keep their hands in the plane of the ball.

6. Defender X3 must stay in interception distance of 3 or 4. He can watch 1 to determine where he thinks the pass will go. Most high school players will look where they are passing when facing double-team pressure.

7. Players 3 and 4 cannot move to receive the pass.

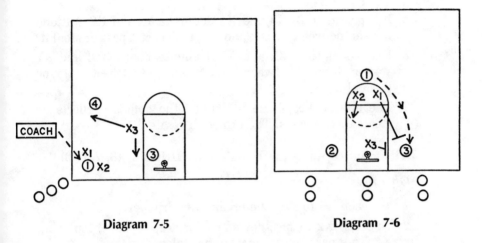

Diagram 7-5   Diagram 7-6

8. After the successful double-team, 1 tries to pass to either 3 or 4; X3 tries to intercept. Player 1 may not lob the ball, he must throw a bounce pass or a direct pass.

Drill 116: Continuous Trapping and Shooting the Gap (6, 7, 8)

Objectives:

1. To teach defenders how to double-team the ball.
2. To teach a gap shooter how to anticipate a pass and get at least a hand on the pass.
3. To teach attackers how to fake a pass and how to successfully complete passes.

Procedure:

1. Line players up as shown in Diagram 7-6.
2. Rotate from offense to defense to end of the line. First player in each of the three lines becomes the new offense.
3. Start by letting 1 have the ball. No offensive player can move. X1 and X2 double-team 1, trying to keep their hands in the plane of the ball. Defender X3 stations himself between 2 and 3, anticipating the pass.
4. If X3 can steal or deflect the pass from 1 to either 2 or 3, X3 does so. If X3 cannot get his hands on the ball, he must get to the new receiver as the ball arrives.

5. If 1 passes to 3, X3 and X1 double-team and X2 stations himself between 1 and 2, hoping to deflect a pass or steal it.

6. If 1 passes to 2, X2 and X3 double-team the ball and X1 stations himself between 1 and 3, hoping to deflect a pass or to steal it.

7. The offense keeps the ball until the defense deflects or steals three passes. Then they all rotate.

Drill 117: Stopping the Breakaway Dribbler (6, 7, 8, 9)

Objectives:

1. To teach X4 to stop the breakaway dribbler.

2. To teach X2 to race downfloor for deep defense, replacing X4. This pass can frequently be stolen.

3. To teach proper defensive rotation in case of a defensive breakdown.

4. To teach trapping in case X1 and X4 trap.

5. To teach the offensive looping dribble technique.

Procedure:

1. Line up players as shown in Diagram 7-7.

2. Rotate from offense to defense; then put X1, 1, X2, and 2 in the backline and 3, X3, 4, and X4 in the front line. Then bring out eight more players.

3. This drill is also good for preventing the fast-break lay-up. Often, we can gain a steal by forcing one more pass.

4. Player X4 makes himself as big as possible as he approaches the dribbler, 1. Player X4 pushes 1 toward the outside; he tries to deflect any pass made to 4 too early. When X4 sees that X2 can intercept a bounce pass to 4, X4 immediately pressures 1 with his hands high waving from his waist and over his head. This encourages the slow bounce pass. Defender X2 knows that X4 will initially induce the bounce pass, and he prepares himself for it. After X2 has had time to recover, X4 will want to keep his hands in the same plane of the ball. Player X4 might deflect the ball as it comes out of the passer's hand.

5. Many times X4 can hedge toward the breakaway dribbler, slowing the dribbler down, allowing the dribbler's defender to recover and stop the dribbler himself.

6. When 4 sees X4 go to pick up 1, 4 breaks toward the goal.
7. When X2 sees 1 driving by X1, X2 sprints downfloor to cover 4. If there had been a defender, X3, and the coach can activate 3, he should sink toward the goal and help. However, the weakside defenders, X4 and X2 in Diagram 7-7, are always responsible for the proper rotation. Player X1 could help X4 trap 1; X1 could rotate around and pick up 2 should the defense successfully halt the dribble penetration.
8. You can alter the drill by letting X2 and X1 run and jump until 1 or 2 drives around X2 and X1.

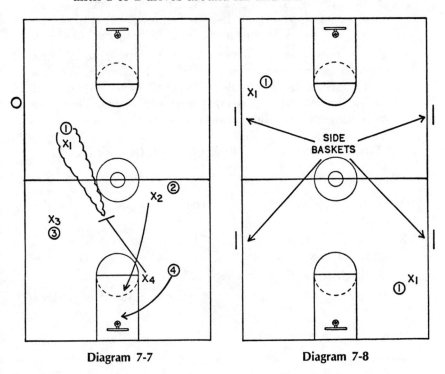

Diagram 7-7   Diagram 7-8

Drill 118: One-on-One Full-Court Game (6, 7, 8, 9)

Objectives:

1. To condition players to full-court press and to attack full-court pressure.
2. To teach aggressive offense and defense.
3. To teach all phases of one-on-one full-court offensive and defensive play.

4. To teach the physical play involved in contesting for a rebound.

Procedure:

1. Line up two players in each sideways, full-court situation as shown in Diagram 7-8.
2. These two, 1 and X1, play one-on-one, playing from side court to side court.
3. After X1 scores (or 1 scores), 1 (or X1) must toss the ball off of the backboard to inbounds the ball. The defender can challenge for the carom, he can full-court press after the carom, or the defender can retreat to half-court defense.
4. The game continues to ten. Whenever either scores, the other must inbound the ball off of the backboard. When a shot is missed, the rebounder brings ball down the floor, and the drill continues until ten points are scored. Then two more players are rotated onto the court.

Drill 119: One-on-One-on-One-on-One-on-One (6, 7, 8, 9)

Objectives:

1. To teach defenders to play good one-on-one pressure defense.
2. To teach instant conversion from offense to defense and from defense to offense.
3. To teach contesting for a rebound.
4. To teach good ball-handling techniques under tremendous pressure.
5. To teach defensive conditioning.

Procedure:

1. Line up players as shown in Diagram 7-9.
2. Both sides of the court are played the same so we will only explain one side. Player 1 attacks and 2 defends.
3. If 1 scores, 2 goes to end of line at basket where 1 scored. The first person in line, 3 in Diagram 7-9, grabs the ball out of the net and prepares to attack 1; 3 has no teammate. So to throw the ball in bounds, 3 must toss the ball off the backboard. Both 3 and 1 can fight for this inbounds pass (rebound). If 3 gets the carom, he attacks 1 to the other end of the court. If 1 gets the rebound, 1 attacks 3 at that basket.

4. If 1 misses, 2 rebounds and attacks 1 to the other end of the court. If 2 scores, 1 goes to the end of the line behind 5; 4 grabs the ball out of the net and tosses it off the backboard (the throw-in). The drill continues until one player scores three consecutive baskets. You could also require more consecutive scores, but the drill will require longer time.

5. You can play until one player scores 10, 12, or 15 points. In this case the points do not have to be consecutive.

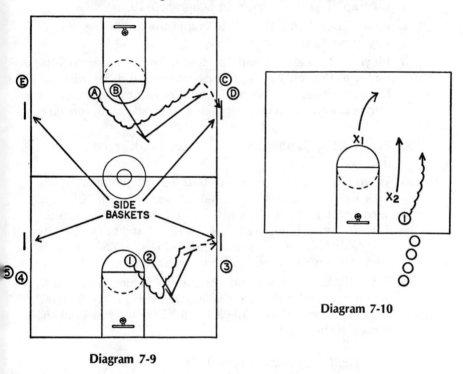

Diagram 7-9

Diagram 7-10

Drill 120: Trapping a Fanned Dribbler (6, 7, 8)

Objectives:

1. To teach X2 to fan the dribbler outside. Most man-to-man presses force the dribbler outside before trapping or stunting.

2. To teach both X1 (trapper) and X2 (container) to stop the attacking dribbler. When X2 stops the dribbler, X1 traps (Give the Outside, Take It Away). When X1 stops the dribbler, X2 traps (The Peel Down). See Procedure 5. for explanation.

3. To teach defenders how to force the dribbler to execute the dribbling reverse.

4. To teach the proper approach and double-team stance.

5. To teach good offensive dribble maneuvering under pressure.

Procedure:

1. Line up players as shown in Diagram 7-10.

2. Rotate from 1 to X1 to X2 to end of the line. First man in line becomes the new 1.

3. Player X2 covers 1 about two feet in front and toward the center of the court (the proper cushion will differ with different players, relative speed, and quickness between the dribbler and the defender being the optimum consideration).

4. Player X1 stays ahead of the ball as it is advanced down the floor.

5. When the defensive man wants to cut off the dribbler, he does so. This occurs two different ways. When X2 races ahead of 1 and cuts him off, we call it Give the Outside, Take It Away. When X1 races ahead of 1 and comes back to cut the dribbler off, we call it The Peel Down. You, as coach, must determine which stunt you want to run.

6. When the dribbler is cut off, the double-teamer races over to double-team with the other defensive man. Player 1 should keep his dribble alive while X2 and X1 try to force 1 out the corner of the court.

Drill 121: Leftfielder's Drill (6, 7, 8, 9)

Objectives:

1. To teach defending the out-of-bounds passer.

2. To teach defending the inbounds receiver.

3. To teach drawing the charge on a cutter, and drawing the charge or forcing a violation on a downcourt receiver.

4. To teach switching when passed up by a pass: Defender X3 picking up 1 and X1 switching to 3 in Diagram 7-11.

5. To teach passing and receiving offensively under extreme defensive pressure.

Procedure:

1. Line up players as shown in Diagram 7-11. Go downcourt and back before rotating positions.

2. Rotate from 1 to X1 to 2 to X2 to 3 to X3 to end of the line. First player in line becomes the new 1.

3. Player 1 has ball and must pass to 2. If 2 breaks toward the passer, 1, X2 might draw the charge, illustrating drawing a charge on a cutter.

4. If 2 likes, he may race downfloor for a baseball pass (not shown in Diagram 7-11). Defender X3 would then attempt to draw a charge on the looking-backward pass receiver; X2 would have to switch to 3. If X3 could not draw the charge, he would force the violation or slow down the next pass by arriving to 2 as the ball arrives.

5. Defender X1 would play the passer, trying to force the bad or hurried pass.

6. If 1 passes to 2, 1 exchanges responsibilities with 2 (as shown in Diagram 7-11). Defender X1 tries to draw the charge on the cutting 1; X3 could try to draw the charge, or as 2 throws the long lob or baseball pass, he could try to intercept that pass. If X3 elects to guard 1, X3 and X1 would exchange assignments, or X3 could elect to stay with his own man, compelling X1 to guard 1. Player X3 must read whether to cover the cutting 1 or stay with his assignment, 3 in Diagram 7-11. Defensive player X2, under any of the above conditions, would try to force 2 to throw an errant pass by guarding the passing shoulder of 2.

7. Player 2, in the beginning, cannot dribble after receiving a pass from 1. After learning the run-and-jump drills, 2 can dribble or pass.

Drill 122: Three-on-Three Denial, Face-Guard, Shortstop, and Centerfield (7, 8)

Objectives:

1. To teach a small number of players in a smaller area so the coach can see and correct defensive mistakes on entering the ball inbounds more quickly.

2. To teach defenders all the techniques of denial, face-guard, shortstop, and centerfield.

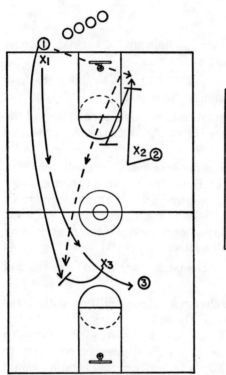

Diagram 7-11

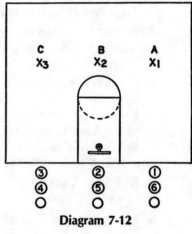

Diagram 7-12

3. To teach attackers how to attack a press.

4. To require defenders to quickly pick up their men as they would have to during a game.

5. To teach any three men defensive stunts that may be part of your defensive team repertoire.

6. To condition players to play the full-court defensive game.

7. To develop instinctive defensive reactions.

8. To develop aggressive defenders.

Procedure:

1. Line up players as shown in Diagram 7-12.

2. Players A, B, and C begin the drill by attacking X1, X2, and X3 at half-court level.

3. If A, B, and C score, they immediately take the ball out-of-bounds. We usually have the player in the center line take the ball out-of-bounds. He is to pass it inbounds to either of his two teammates. These three immediately attack the

goal again. Because A, B, and C scored, X1, X2, and X3 go to the end of the line. Players 1, 2, and 3 race onto the floor, ready to deny the inbounds pass from B to either A or C. The coach can specify which cut or screening maneuvers (usually the maneuver used by the next opponent) he wants used. He may also call for 2, X2, or B to use shortstopping, leftfielding, or centerfield techniques.

4. If A, B, or C miss and X1, X2, or X3 gets the defensive rebound, then X2 would take the ball-out-of-bounds and pass it to X1 or X3. Again, 1, 2, and 3 would have to hurry onto the court into denial position on X1, X2, and X3. The coach can assign cuts, screens, and defensive movements he wants the offense or the defense to use.

5. As the season progresses we will use the three-on-three drill over the entire court. By placing three men out-of-bounds on each end line, we have a continuous three-on-three full-court game (see Drill 151). But we change the rules slightly. The team that scores stays on the court and plays defense. The three out-of-bounds men become the new offense.

6. When we switch to full-court, we require the attackers to receive the inbounds pass below the free throw line, and all offensive players must remain below the advancement of the ball. This gives us no offensive clearouts, enabling us to work on any or all of our three-man defensive stunts.

7. You may, instead of allowing the scoring team to keep the ball, require them to go on defense. This would send the defensive team off the court, and it would mandate 1, 2, and 3 as the next attackers. This simulates exactly what happens in ball games, but it does not reward the offensive team for scoring.

8. You could combine the drill with Drill 151. If the team of A, B, and C scores, they go on defense. Players 1, 2, and 3 enter the floor and X1, X2, and X3 go to the end of the line. If A, B, and C stop 1, 2, and 3, they stay on offense while 4, 5, and 6 come out to stop A, B, and C. If 1, 2, and 3 score, A, B, and C would go off the court. 1, 2, and 3 go on defense against 5, 4, and 6.

Drill 123: Run-and-Jump Exchange Drill (7, 8)

Objectives:

1. To teach defensive communication.
2. To teach proper and instant rotation.

3. To teach continuous "jump," "used," and "trap" reactions.

4. To teach techniques of run and jumping, double-teaming, and leaving the attacker who has lost his dribble.

5. To teach the "fishhook" route of run-and-jump defenders.

Procedure:

1. Line up players as shown in Diagram 7-13.

2. Rotate from 1 to X1 to X2 to end of the line after completing a trip downfloor and back. First man in line becomes the new 1.

3. Player 1 attacks down the floor and back but cannot dribble out of his lane. Players X1 and X2 defend.

4. Defender X2 can yell "jump," which will force X1 to run the "fishhook" looking for the open man; X2 can yell "trap," forcing X1 to help trap; X2 would follow "trap" with "used," again sending X1 to find the open attacker (fishhook route). "Used" is used when 1 picks up his dribble. After "used," 1 must wait three seconds before he can begin his dribble again. This would allow X1 time to run his route and recover, and it would simulate a pass to a teammate, such as would be used in game conditions.

5. Defender X2 would cut toward X1, and X1 would run at 1 yelling "trap," "jump," or "used" during the second phase of the drill. The third phase would occur as in step 4, the fourth phase would be a repetition of step 5, and so on.

Drill 124: Two-Man Run and Jump (7, 8, 9)

Objectives:

1. To teach defenders to play run-and-jump defense.

2. To condition the athlete for pressure defense and fast-break offense.

3. To improve offensive ball handling under pressure.

Procedure:

1. Line up players in two lines as shown in Diagram 7-14.

2. Rotate from offense to defense to the end of the line. First players in both lines become the new attackers.

3. The offense advances the ball down the court and back. Defense stays defense down the floor and back.

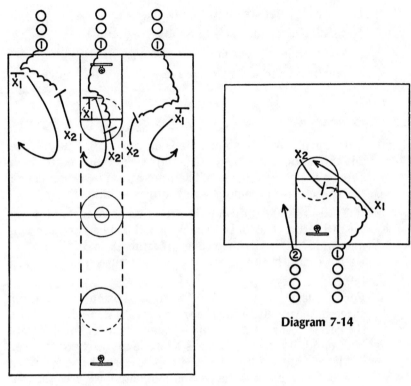

Diagram 7-14

Diagram 7-13

4. Player 1 dribbles but X1 will not let him outside. Player 2 may never get above the ball; X2 may never get below the line of the advancement of the ball.

5. When X2 wants, he runs directly at 1 as X1 forces 1 inside. If 1 continues his dribble, he must charge X2 or veer outside. If 1 picks up the ball to pass to 2, X2 tries to deflect it as X1 races to cover 2 and we continue this run and jump the length of the court and back. If X1 and X2 steal the ball, they fast break. Defenders X1 and X2 hold their double-team as long as 1 continues his dribble. If 1 and 2 cross, X1 and X2 switch, creating the impression of a zone press.

Drill 125: Three-Man Run and Jump (7, 8, 9)

Objectives:

1. To teach three defensive men how to coordinate their efforts in a three-man run and jump.

2. To improve offensive ball handling.

3. To teach proper methods of double-teaming.

4. To teach shooting the gap.

5. To condition the defensive players to play full-court pressure.

Procedures:

1. Line up players as shown in Diagram 7-15. The offense advances the ball downcourt and back, then rotate from offense to defense to end of the line. First player in each of the three lines become the new offensive players.

2. If 2, the middle attacker, is dribbling, he must be going toward either 1 or 3. In either case, that is a two-man run and jump (Drill 124). However, if either 1 or 3 is dribbling we force him to the inside and run our three-man run and jump.

3. For discussion, let's let 1 drive to the inside and run our three-man run and jump (Diagram 7-15). As 1 drives inside, X2 races toward 1 and double-teams with X1 until 1 puts both hands on the ball. This is X1's cue to race hard to cover 3. Meanwhile, X3 has shot the gap between 1 and 2 for the interception. Even if the pass is completed, we are still in a man-to-man press: Player X1 has 3, X2 has 1, and X3 has 2. If the offense should turn the ball over, the defense can fast break. The coach should require that the two offensive men without the ball stay behind the advancement of the ball. That not only expedites teaching but it permits more run and jumps per possession. And time is of utmost importance in the life of a coach.

Drill 126: Three-on-Two Run and Jump (7, 8, 9)

Objectives:

1. To teach three defenders how to run and jump against two attackers.

2. To condition defensively for full-court pressure defense.

3. To teach double-teaming and shooting the gap.

4. To improve the ball handlers offensively.

Procedure:

1. Line up players in two lines as shown in Digram 7-16. The

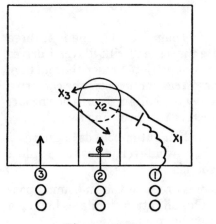

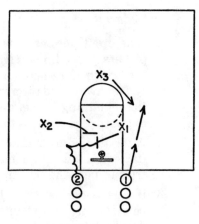

Diagram 7-15   Diagram 7-16

offense advances the ball downcourt and back. Defender X3 starts at safety on the way downcourt and X1 starts at safety on the way back; X2 is the first safety when the two lines rotate after a trip downfloor and back.

2. Players X1 and X2 run and jump while X3 shoots the gap. After X1 and X2 stop 2's dribble, X2 drops and becomes the new short safety, waiting to shoot the gap on the next run and jump.

3. In case of a steal, you can allow a three-on-two fast break.

Drill 127: Three Drill Offensively (7, 8, 9)

Objectives:

1. To teach 2 to catch 1 and either block the shot or foul, preventing the easy lay-up.

2. To teach 2 to pass in-bounds against pressure or denial defense, and to teach 1 to free himself from a denial defender.

3. To teach 3 the proper techniques of face-guard pressure, denial, and sagging.

4. To teach 3 how to delay the two-on-one fast break until defensive help arrives, and to teach 1 and 2 to attack a lone defender.

5. Almost all of our full-court drills are multipurpose, teaching many of the offensive and defensive phases of the full-court game.

Procedure:

1. Line up players as shown in Diagram 7-17. The first three players in the line activate the Three Drill: Player 1 drives the length of the floor for a lay-up; 2 lets 1 reach the foul line, 15 feet away, and then tries to catch him before he can drive the remaining 75 feet and lay the ball in; 3 races downcourt to guard 1 as he tries to receive the throw-in pass.

2. After 1's lay-up, 2 takes the ball out-of-bounds, 3 guards 1 (face-guard, denial, slough, or whatever you want) while 2 tries to pass the ball in-bounds.

3. If 3 face-guards, then 1 must receive the in-bounds pass below the free throw line. This situation simulates having a deeper defender to steal any lob pass.

4. When ball is in-bounded, 1 and 2 fast break while 3 defends.

5. The second group of three players begins their drill when the first group reaches midcourt on their return trip.

Drill 128: Three Drill Defensively (7, 8, 9)

Objectives:

1. To condition defensively.
2. To teach 1 the driving lay-up under pressure.
3. To teach 2 to catch 1 before the lay-up.
4. To teach 2 to keep his dribble alive, the perfect attack against man-to-man full court pressure, against a run-and-jump defense, and against a team defense that is slow setting up its defense.
5. To teach 1 and 3 proper double-teaming techniques, and to teach the two defenders how to control and dominate one attacker.
6. To teach one player how to attack two defenders and either get the good shot or the lay-up.
7. To teach two defenders how to stop the one-on-two fast break.

Procedure:

1. Line up players as in the three drill offensively. It is easy for the players to remember the drills: three drill—three men; offensively (two attackers, one defender), defensively (two defenders, one attacker).

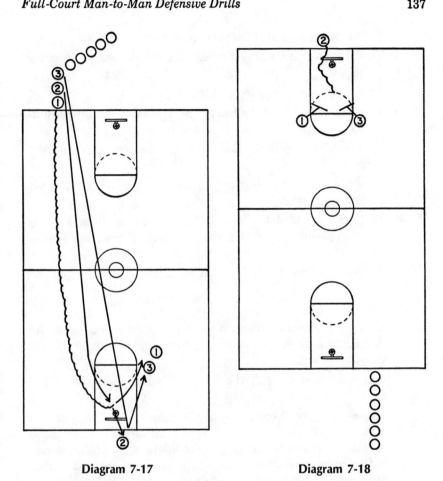

Diagram 7-17   Diagram 7-18

2. Players 1, 2, and 3 perform the same duties on their trip downfloor as they did in the three drill offensively.

3. After 2 gets the rebound, however, he does not throw the ball into 1 because 1 has become a defender. Instead, 2 tries to dribble the length of the court against the repeated double-teams of 1 and 3 (Diagram 7-18).

4. Players 1 and 3 try to force 2 to dribble off the court, exiting by the baseline corner.

Drill 129: Four Drill Defensively (7, 8, 9)

Objectives:

1. To condition defensively.

2. To teach techniques of a two-on-two fast break.

3. To drill on inbounding passes against pressure defenses.

4. To teach two skilled athletes to attack pressure defenses from the out-of-bounds pass to the lay-up.

5. To teach two-on-two full-court play offensively and defensively.

6. To teach player 3 denial, face-guarding, or containment defense.

7. To teach 1 to free himself to receive the inbounds pass against pressure.

8. To teach 3 and 4 tandem defense, full-court man-to-man pressure, double-teaming, run and jump, and other defensive tactics.

9. To teach proper methods of pressuring the inbounds passer.

Procedure:

1. Line up players at the end line to drive the length of the court as in all the three-, four-, five-, and six-drills.

2. Players 1, 2, and 3 have the same responsibilities on their trip downfloor as they did in the other drills (Three Drill Offensively and Three Drill Defensively).

3. Player 4, instead of racing to the baseline and timing his return trip to correspond to 2's passing the ball in to 1 as he would if it were the four drill offensively (Drill 152), defends 2, the inbounds passer. This puts added pressure on 2 to pass successfully inbounds. It also helps drill 2 on inbounding passes against full-court presses (Diagram 7-19.)

4. Once the ball is inbounded, 1 and 2 attack 3 and 4 in a two-on-two fast-break situation or two-on-two run and jumps.

5. Player 3 defends 1 by face-guarding, denial, or slough. Player 4 tries to keep 2 from spotting 1 or from passing cleanly into him.

6. Players 3 and 4 retreat quickly to a tandem defense or they can run and jump, double-team, or use any defense the coach dictates.

7. Players 1 and 2 can screen for each other, weave, pass all the way down the floor, dribble all the way down the floor, or combine the two.

8. You could permit 4 to shortstop (double-team with 3) or play

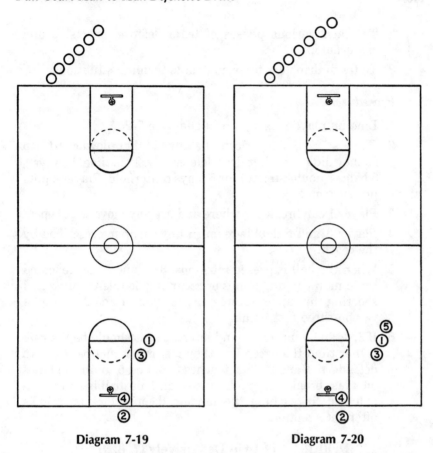

Diagram 7-19   Diagram 7-20

centerfield (play at the free throw line in case of a lob pass to 1).

Drill 130: Five Drill Defensively (7, 8, 9)

Objectives:

1. To condition defensively.
2. To teach 1 to free himself from double-teaming tactics so that he can receive the inbounds pass.
3. To teach 2 to make an accurate inbounds pass against great pressure.
4. To teach fast breaking after making an interception.
5. To teach two attackers to fast break against three defenders.
6. To teach 4 to apply pressure on the out-of-bounds passer.

7. To teach various phases of team defense: shortstop and centerfield.
8. To teach dribblers to avoid double-teaming situations.

Procedure:

1. Line up players as shown in Diagram 7-20.
2. Players 1, 2, and 3 perform the same in their downcourt trip as they did in the four drill defensively. This time, however, 5 helps 3 double-team 1, or 5 plays centerfield. Player 4 puts pressure on 2.
3. Player 1 can break anywhere and use any move to get open.
4. Player 3 and 5 double-team in any manner prescribed by the coach.
5. When the ball is passed inbounds, 3, 4, and 5 run repeated three-man run and jumps or recurring double-teaming and shooting the gap for interception. Players 1 and 2 attempt a two-on-three fast break.
6. If 3, 4, and 5 intercept, and interceptions should be the rule rather than the exception, they fast break against the two defenders, 1 and 2. This teaches 3, 4, and 5 to fill the lanes on a fast break after making a steal. This drill is an invaluable aid to teaching the tandem defense for fast breaks after interceptions.

Drill 131: Six Drill Defensively (7, 8, 9)

Objectives:

1. To condition players for the full-court pressure defense.
2. To teach denial, face-guarding, shortstopping, and centerfielding tactics of full-court pressure defense.
3. To teach fast-break offense and defense.
4. To teach run-and-jump defense, and to teach double-teaming and shooting the gap.

Procedure:

1. Line up players at the end of the court as in Diagram 7-21. They are to run the length of the court before returning as explained below.
2. Players 1, 2, 3, and 4 perform the same maneuvers as they did in the Three Drill Offensively and Defensively, in the

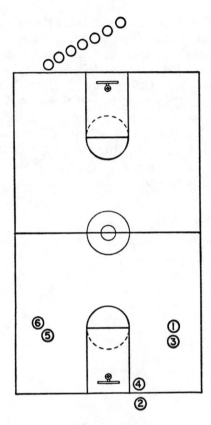

Diagram 7-21

Four Drill Defensively, and the Five Drill Defensively on
their trip downcourt. Player 6, however, races downcourt to
the endline, and then comes inbounds to receive a pass from
2; 5, instead of shortstopping or centerfielding as he did in
the Five Drill Defensively, defends against 6.

3. Player 4 can pressure the inbound passer or he can drop off
   2 and play shortstop or centerfield.
4. If the ball is inbounded to either 1 or 6, 3, 4, and 5 have the
   option of double-teaming the ball and shooting the gap, or
   they can run repeated run and jumps the length of the
   court. If the offense gets free, a fast-break tandem defense
   must quickly be formed. If an interception occurs, the fast
   break should go the other way; and the drill begins from the
   far baseline again.
5. As stated before, the Three Drills Offensively and Defensively, the Four Drills Offensively and Defensively, the

Five Drills Offensively and Defensively, and the Six Drills Offensively and Defensively all go together. Players 1, 2, 3, for example, perform the same duties in the Four Drills Offensively (Drill 152) and Defensively (Drill 129), and in the Five Drills Offensively (Drill 153) and Defensively (Drill 130). Players 4, 5, and 6 may have to adjust their duties. This makes it easy for the players to learn and to execute. The first player in line is 1, the second player is 2, and so on. These men run the length of the court, score a lay-up, then begin the drills on their way back downcourt. This simulates scoring, then quickly converting to defense.

8

Full-Court Zone-Press Defensive Drills

Zone-press drills, by the very nature of what they intend to teach, must be more structured, more defined, more specific. They must, if they are to achieve their purposes, provide drilling on that structure. The first ten drills are not specific to any one type zone press; they would help develop any zone press. The last three drills are much more specific: They provide drilling only for the diamond press (the 1-2-1-1 or 1-2-2). But even the last three drills can be adjusted by you to teach the box press (2-2-1) or the 2-1-2 or any other zone press that appeals to you. To adjust these three drills, the coach uses the same objectives and procedures. He simply places his personnel differently. He puts his defenders in the positions of the alignment of his chosen press, and he places his attackers in the holes and seams of that zone press. By following the same objectives and procedures already outlined in Drills 142, 143, and 144, the coach can teach his specific zone press.

Drill 132: Wave Drill (7, 8, 9)

Objectives:

1. To teach press defenders to race sideways to cover a player cutting deep.
2. To teach coordination and balance.
3. To teach interception of long passes.
4. To teach the baseball pass.

Procedure:

1. Line up players as shown in Diagram 8-1.
2. Rotate from passer to defender to end of the line. First player in line becomes the next defender.

3. Coach stands where X1, X2, and X3 can see him.

4. Coach signals the direction the defender is to race sideways.

5. After a few swing steps by the defenders, 1, 2, and 3 throw a baseball pass that X1, X2, and X3 must intercept. After the reception, X1, X2, and X3 dribble the ball hard back downcourt and pass to the second player in line.

6. Players 1, 2, and 3 step out as the next X1, X2, and X3; and the drill continues.

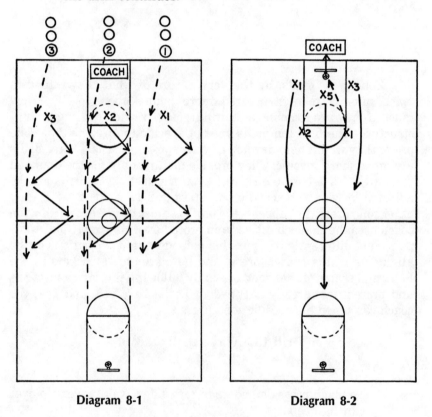

Diagram 8-1   Diagram 8-2

Drill 133: Intercept Drill (8)

Objectives:

1. To teach instant conversion from offense to a defensive press.

2. To teach defenders to intercept quickly thrown-in passes, lob passes, or long passes.

Procedures:

1. Line up players as shown in Diagram 8-2.
2. Players X1, X2, X3, X4, and X5 run an offensive play. One of the players shoots. All players go to their assignment: one and one-half to safety defense and three to the offensive boards for an offensive rebound.
3. After X1, X2, X3, X4, or X5 score, they race to their press positions (2-2-1 zone press in Diagram 8-2). Coach grabs the ball out of the net and tosses a semilob baseball pass into a defender's area. The defender intercepts; passes to a teammate ahead of him. When the interception is turned into a score (you could have your team reset the ball up at the half-court level, and shoot again), the defenders hustle to their respective defensive positions. The coach grabs the ball and throws a semilob baseball pass, and the drill continues.

Drill 134: Never-Too-Late Drill (7, 8, 9)

Objectives:

1. To teach X1 to recover and intercept a pass. This shows defenders they are never too late.
2. To teach X5 when to cover the outside jumper.
3. To teach 1 and 2 to attack one defender.

Procedures:

1. Line up players as shown in Diagram 8-3.
2. Rotate from X1 to 1 to X5 to 2 to end of the line.
3. Players 1 and 2 begin at the 28-foot mark. Player 2 initiates the drill with a dribble that tells 1, 2, and X1 to begin moving toward the basket.
3. Player X1 starts behind midcourt. He takes the shortest route toward the defensive goal. Players 1 and 2 attack X5.
4. When X5 sees that X1 has recovered sufficiently to intercept any pass directed toward 1, he challenges 2's jump shot, spreading himself, cutting 2 baseline and forcing him to throw a lob or bounce pass. Defender X1 must intercept this pass. If 2 drives baseline, X1 must draw the charge while X5 attempts to block the shot.

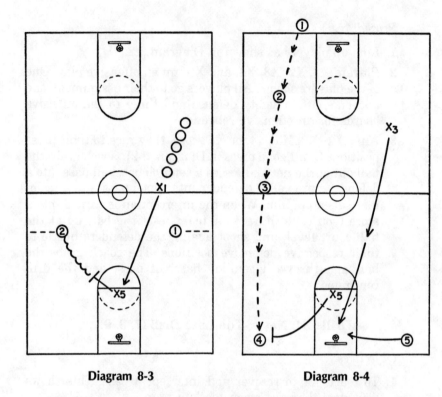

Diagram 8-3   Diagram 8-4

Drill 135: Two-Man and Team Recovery Drills (7, 8, 9)

Objectives:

1. To teach that proper recovery never allows a lay-up. The defenders quickly see that they are never too late if they hustle.
2. To teach X5 to intercept long passes.
3. To teach X5 to stay home until he sees that X3 can recover to the basket area.
4. To teach two-on-two and three-on-two safety coverages.
5. To teach defensive movement while passes are in the air.

Procedures:

1. Line up five offensive players and two defenders as shown in Diagram 8-4.
2. Player 1 passes to 2 who passes to 3 who passes to 4. All of these passes are rapid, thrown as soon as they are received.

3. Player X3 begins to race downfloor as 1 passes to 2.

4. When 4 receives the ball, X5 goes out to cover him. Player 5 breaks to the basket for a pass from 4. Player X3 must get to the basket before 5 gets there; X3 should be able to deflect or steal any pass from 4 to 5.

5. Alternate passing route: When 2 receives the ball he can bypass 3 and pass directly to either 4 or 5. When 3 receives the pass he can pass to 5 as well as 4. This keeps X5 honest. It also allows X5 to practice being a long-pass interceptor. If 5 receives a pass, 4 breaks to the basket. Defender X3 must prevent a pass to 4 for the lay-up should 5 receive a pass from 3 or 2.

6. Players 4 and 5 can play two-on-two against X3 and X5. Player 3 can break to the head of the circle and make the drill and three-on-two after the safety drills have been learned.

7. Diagram 8-5 depicts a full-court team recovery drill. You can make a baseball pass to either 4 or 5. All team members must arrive to half-court defensive stations before 4 can pass to 5.

Drill 136: Trap, Hedge, and Switch Drill (7, 8)

Objectives:

1. To teach two defenders how to trap.

2. To teach an attacker the step-through move and how to pass out of a successful trap.

3. To teach hedging yet recovering to intercept a pass.

4. To teach run and jump or a defensive switch with the container intercepting the habit pass.

Procedure:

1. Line up players as shown in Diagram 8-6.

2. Rotate from 5 to X5 to X1 to 1 to 2 to X2 to X3 to 3 to 6 to X6 to X4 to 4 to the end of the line. First player in line becomes the next 5.

3. Players 1, 2, and 4 begin the drill by dribbling. Players X1, X2, and X4 pressure 1, 2, and 4.

4. When X5, X3, and X6 want, they sprint toward the dribbling 1, 2, and 4.

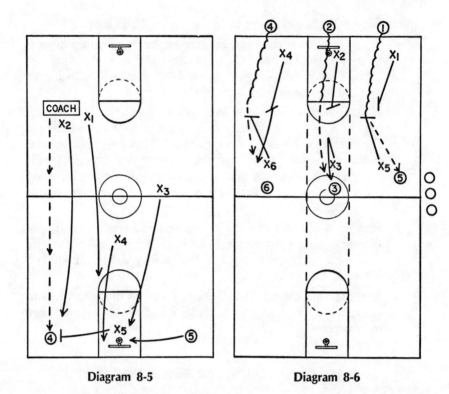

Diagram 8-5   Diagram 8-6

5. Defender X5 yells "trap," and X5 and X1 trap 1; 1 keeps his dribble alive. Finally, when 1 is trapped, 1 will use his step-through move to pass to 5.

6. Meanwhile, X3 has "hedged" toward 2. When 2 sees X3 coming, 2 passes to 3; X3 must get back toward 3 and at least deflect this pass.

7. Meanwhile, X6 has "jumped" toward 4. When 4 sees X6 coming, 4 passes to 6. When X4 hears X6 call "jump," X4 races to get into the passing lane between 4 and 6. X4 must get a hand on the pass from 4 to 6.

Drill 137: Sideline Double-Team Drill (8)

Objectives:

1. To teach sideline trapping; the sidelines are the areas where the most zone-press traps occur.

2. To teach hustling to trap again after being passed up by the ball.

3. To teach the slides of your zone press.

4. To teach recovering without allowing an easy shot.

5. To teach passing out of a trap.

Procedure:

1. Line up players as shown in Diagram 8-7.

2. Rotate players so that all candidates for a particular position will get drilling at that position.

3. Coach begins drill by passing ball into 1. Defenders X2 and X3 trap 1; X4 plays short safety and X5 plays deep safety.

4. Player 1 passes to 2. Defender X4 must allow this pass during the drill. During a game, X4 would intercept if possible.

5. Players X3 and X4 trap 2; X2 covers the horizontal passing lane, and X5 still plays safety.

6. Player 2 passes to 3. Defenders X4 and X5 trap 3; X2 must get back in time to stop the pass to 4 for a score; X3 retreats to high-post defense.

7. These are the basic trapping slides of the 1-2-1-1 full-court zone press. The same type slides can be worked out for your favorite zone press.

8. You can allow the passes from 1 to 2 to 3 to be quick or slow. When slow, you should stress learning the slides; when quick, you should stress proper recovery.

9. You could even allow a skip pass, allowing 1 to pass all the way downcourt to 3. The defense must react properly.

10. You could allow 2 to pass to either 3 or 4. This would require X5 to read before going for his coverage, teaching what the deep safety must do in all zone presses. This also requires X2 to read before making his coverage.

Drill 138: Throwback Pass Drill (8)

Objectives:

1. To teach proper ways of trapping.

2. To teach proper spacing and gapping.

3. To teach shooting the gaps for steals.

4. To teach throwback coverage rules of your zone press.

5. To teach all the basic assignments of your zone press.

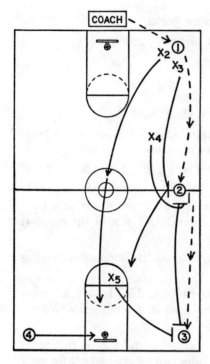

Diagram 8-7

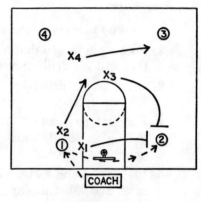

Diagram 8-8

Procedure:

1. Line up four attackers at four corners of backcourt, using the 28-foot markers and the baseline as the bases of the rectangle.

2. Put four defenders in a diamond formation as shown in Diagram 8-8.

3. The coach stands out-of-bounds and passes into either 2 or 1 (1 in Diagram 8-8).

4. Player 1 tries to escape X1 and X2's trap (can activate Drill 114).

5. Once 1's dribble has been stopped, X3 and X4 gap 2, 3, and 4. A pass from 1 to 2 (short throwback) or a pass from 1 to 3 (long throwback) would represent a throwback pass.

6. Player 1 passes to 2 in Diagram 8-8, a short throwback pass because it is in front of X3; X3 contains 2 while X1 comes to trap with X3. While the pass in in the air, X4 gaps 3 and 4, shading toward 3, and X2 gaps 1 and 4, shading toward 4.

7. A pass from 1 to 3 (Diagram 8-9) illustrates a long throwback because it occurs behind X3, the front-gap shooter. Defender X4 arrives at the same time as 3 receives the ball. This frees X3 to try for the interception. If X3 cannot intercept, X4 must contain 3 until X3 can help trap. Defenders X1 and X2 rotate to their new positions while the pass is in the air.

8. A pass from 1 to 4 is not a throwback. It is a vertical attacking pass. But this pass can also be ruled and drilled on in this drill if you wish. A pass from 1 to 4 would have X4 containing 4 and X2 helping X4 trap (not shown in the diagrams). Defender X3 would rotate to the downcourt vertical passing lane as X2 did in Diagram 8-9. Player X1 would rotate to the new diagonal passing lane as he did in Diagram 8-9.

9. Passes can continue back and forth, especially between 1 and 2 until all defenders know their throwback-coverage assignments instinctively. Drilling on this drill daily during the early preseason practice sessions pays great dividends during the later season.

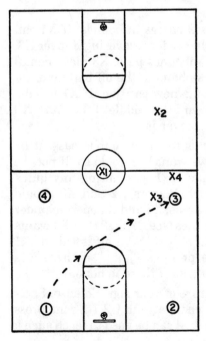

Diagram 8-9

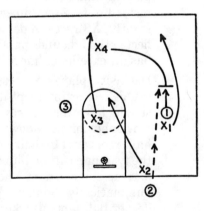

Diagram 8-10

Drill 139: Rotation from Face-Guard Zone Press (7, 8)

Objectives:

1. To teach basic face-guarding pressure even when running a zone press.
2. To teach players to react to the command "ball" (or whatever you use to signal the ball has been passed inbounds).
3. To teach defenders how to get to their new positions when the ball is thrown over the head of a face-guarding defender.
4. To teach defenders to go from zone to man-to-man or from zone to zone in the pressure defenses.

Procedure:

1. Line players up as shown in Diagram 8-10.
2. Rotate so that every defensive candidate for X1, X2, X3, and X4 get to practice their positions in your zone press.
3. Defender X2 covers 2; X1 and X3 face-guard while X4 covers short safety. You can bring X2 off of 2 and let X2 play shortstop or centerfield.
4. Defender X2 yells "ball" as 2 passes in bounds. If X1 can deflect the pass, we have a chance for recovering. Player X3, playing denial, can see the inbounds pass. X3 plays denial instead of face-guard because he is in the off-ball lane. Instantly, X3 races to defend his new position. If X1 has deflected the inbounds pass toward the middle of the court, X3 has an excellent chance to recover it.
5. Defensive player X4 responds to the inbounds pass. If he can deflect or intercept it, we want him to do so. If not, he should have instant coverage on 1, preventing any quick movement or pass downcourt. Players X2 and X3 should have recovered to their new areas; X1 and X4 operate under the two-man run-and-jump rules (see Drill 124). If X4 wants a "trap" or a "jump," he calls it. If nothing is called, X1 automatically "jumps." We prefer a "jump" if there is a deeper ball-lane attacker; a trap if there is none.
6. Traps can change the structure of your zone defense. Face-guarding, for instance, can change your 1-2-1-1 zone press into a 2-2-1 zone press. This drill can be used to teach such a coverage.

Drill 140: Four-on-Three Press (7, 8, 9)

Objectives:

1. To teach face-guard, denial, shortstopping, and centerfield techniques of preventing the entrance pass.
2. To teach trapping and shooting-the-gap techniques once the ball has entered the court.
3. To teach run and jumps and other stunts as the ball is advanced down the floor (man or zone).
4. To teach the slides and the trapping mechanics of your zone press.
5. To teach safety defense should the attackers manage to get the ball up-court.
6. To teach fast-break techniques should the defenders intercept a pass or recover a missed shot.
7. To teach instant conversion from offense to defense and from defense to offense.
8. To teach handling of the basketball under extreme defensive pressure.

Procedure:

1. Line up players as shown in Diagram 8-11. X4 would locate differently depending upon your defensive strategy.
2. Player X4 can play centerfield, can shortstop, can double on 1, etc.
3. Once the ball is entered, you can trap, force a run and jump, play the slides of your zone press, etc.
4. Players 1, 2, and 3 attack X1, X2, X3, and X4 to the other end of the court. If the defense forces a turnover, they fast break against 1, 2, and 3.
5. If 1, 2, and 3 manage to get the ball downcourt and miss a shot, X1, X2, X3, and X4 rebound and fast break against 1, 2, and 3.
6. If 1, 2, and 3 score, they line up at the far end of the court, and they repeat the process they performed at the near end.
7. Make sure all potential candidates for the X1, X2, X3, and X4 positions in whatever defense you choose to run get to drill on those positions.

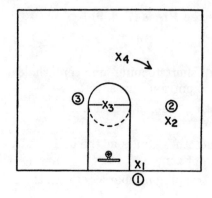

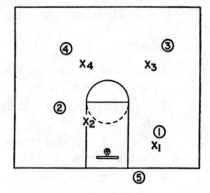

Diagram 8-11   Diagram 8-12

Drill 141: Full-Court Horseshoe Drill (8)

Objectives:

1. To learn all the team tactics, slides, and rules of your favorite zone press.
2. To learn floor positioning, proper floats, and proper spacing.
3. To learn to recognize the passing lanes.
4. To understand the proper team rotations on all slides, stunts, etc.

Procedure:

1. Line up four offensive players in each of the four corners in the backcourt. Place one player out-of-bounds. He inbounds the ball.
2. Line up four backcourt defenders in the alignment of your full-court zone press. In Diagram 8-12 your zone press is the 2-2-1 face-guard. If you run a 1-2-1-1 zone press, you adjust the drill by placing the offense into a 1-2-1 shell set and put X1 on the out-of-bounds passer. You could allow X3 to face-guard 1 and X4 to gap 3 and 4. This allows harassment of the inbounds pass.
3. You can work on any of the following, mix up two or three, or work on all of them.
   a. Get ball in bounds against face-guard or denial: Players X1 and X2 face-guard or deny while X3 and X4 play centerfield.

b. Let X1 and X2 shortstop 1, forcing the ball to 2, and then pressing.

c. Allow X1 and X3 to exchange places on a lobbed in-bounds pass (X2 and X4 if ball is thrown into 2). As the ball flies toward 1, X3 comes hard, arriving to 1 as the ball arrives. Player X1 rotates to second line of the defense.

d. Run any stunt once the ball is inbounded: run and jump, give outside then take it away, peel back, basic traps of your zone press, etc.

e. Permit only passing, including passing back out-of-bounds. This forces defenders to run their slides as the ball floats through the air.

f. Make any throwback or vertical pass, requiring defenders to know your throwback rules (short and long).

g. Allow 1 or 2 to dribble drive, forcing the weakside deep defender to stop the breakaway dribbler.

Drill 142: Drilling the Point and Short Safety of the Diamond Press (8)

Objectives:

1. To teach your point man to keep arms over the shoulder of the passer.
2. To teach your short safety to intercept the lob pass.
3. To teach the baseball pass under pressure.

Procedure:

1. Line up players as shown in Diagram 8-13. Be sure all candidates for the X1 and X4 positions receive extensive drilling.
2. The man with the ball runs along the baseline intending to throw the pass inbounds to the men at half-court.
3. Defender X1 follows the ball, keeping pressure on the throwing arm of the passer. Most high school players must point their shoulder in the direction of the throw; they must put their foot opposite from their throwing arm forward. Defender X1 must force the lob pass if X4 is to have any chance for an interception. Defender X1 might force the passer to pass off balance.

4. Player X4 reads the feet and the eyes of the passer; he keeps readjusting his position (such as when the ball is on the right side, X4 shades to the right), intending to intercept the pass.

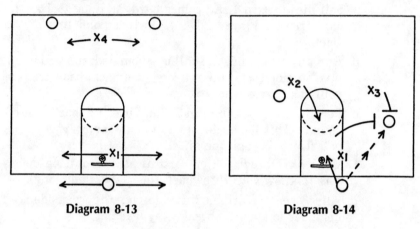

Diagram 8-13   Diagram 8-14

Drill 143: Drilling the Front Three of the Diamond Press (8)

Objectives:

1. To teach timing needed by the front three defenders on the 1-2-2 zone press.
2. To teach proper double-teaming and shooting the gap.
3. To teach passing under defensive pressure.
4. To develop conditioning, especially as the season progresses.

Procedure:

1. Line up players as shown in Diagram 8-14. Be sure all players who are trying for the point and wing positions get enough drilling at these positions.
2. Out-of-bounds player may throw pass into either receiver. Out-of-bounds player then steps in bounds.
3. The two players designated to double-team do that and the other wing man becomes the interceptor.
4. You can alter the diamond alignment yet run the diamond traps; you could drop X1 off the out-of-bounds passer, letting X1 shortstop, play centerfield, etc.

5. You can allow the players to advance the ball all the way downcourt, running continuous traps and shooting the gaps or running a stunt, such as a run and jump.

Drill 144: Overload-the-Diamond Traps (6, 8)

Objectives:

1. To teach the interceptor to know his coverage responsibilities.
2. To teach interception (proper spacing) of passes into passing-lane coverages.
3. To teach the double-team stance.
4. To teach proper passing under great defensive pressure.

Procedure:

1. Line up players as shown in Diagram 8-15.
2. Be sure that all personnel playing X1, X2, X3, X4 and X5 get to drill on their positions.

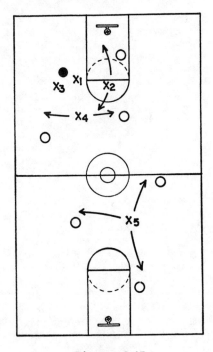

Diagram 8-15

3. The double-team in Diagram 8-15 is set in the corner by the point and the wing man, X1 and X3. You can alter these double-team positions to cover the trapping areas of your zone press.

4. The other defenders are set between two or more offensive players.

5. The offensive man with the ball may pass to either offensive receiver. The receivers may not move toward the ball to receive it.

6. The interceptors watch the legs and the eyes of the passer in an attempt to steal the pass. The legs and the eyes usually point in the direction of the pass.

7. You can alter the drill by requiring X1 and X3 to stop the ball-handler's dribble before passing takes place (see Drill 114).

8. You can also move the drill to the areas of your half-court zone traps; or you can change the areas of the traps to correspond to the areas of your favorite full-court zone press.

9

Transition
Defensive Drills

Transitional basketball, better known by many coaches as fast-break basketball, is a major directional movement of the modern game. It not only includes the fast break and defense of the fast break, but it involves all the different types of pressure. It is quick conversion from offense to defense and from defense to offense. In essence, it is the full-court game, the 90-foot game.

How quickly a player can convert from offense to defense or from defense to offense often spells victory of defeat for his team. Most coaches drill long and laboriously on conversion from defense to offense: on pressing and stealing, then fast breaking with the ball. However, precious few coaches place equal emphasis on converting from offense to defense when a steal occurs. Yet in the final score, a basket saved is as important as a basket scored.

Because less emphasis is placed on the defensive transition during practice sessions, your fast break scores easily during practice. But when faced with a stiffer and a more knowledgeable transitional defense, your fast break will often bog down during a tough game. But by drilling equally as hard on transitional defense, your transitional defense will improve your transitional offense. And when your transitional offense faces these more knowledgeable transitional roadblocks, they will not only improve more rapidly but they will be more ready for the tougher game situations. Only a few successful tough possessions are needed to supply victory in these close contests. This alone is major reason for stressing transitional defense.

All ten drills in this chapter aim to teach the player to instinctively and quickly react from offense to defense. These include the quick offensive turnover that impels your attacker to become an instant defender and to stop the inevitable onslaught.

Another often overlooked phase of transitional defense is the safety defense at the end of a press. Your opponents will sometimes break your press, but your team should have built-in mechanisms to still stop an easy shot even when badly outnumbered by the team that has just broken your press. Often the defense only has to delay the shot a pass or two until full defensive help arrives. Several drills in this chapter develop this type of thinking.

The ten drills in this chapter coupled with the 42 previous multipurpose drills dealing with transitional defense offer more than enough variety to prevent late-season staleness. Although all 52 teach many different ideas and techniques, they all have one central theme, one fundamental concept: They all teach transitional defense.

Drill 145: Passing into One-on-One (7, 8, 9)

Objectives:

1. To teach aggressive one-on-one defense and offense.
2. To teach sharp-bounce and chest passing skills.
3. To teach defensive alertness.
4. To condition defensively.
5. To teach fast-break defense by denying the dribbler into the middle lane on the court.

Procedure:

1. Line up players as shown in Diagram 9-1.
2. Have defensive players in alternate positions in each line. By doing this, the drill will allow each group of passers to begin when the group ahead has thrown two passes. Player 1 must aggressively attack the basket or the third group will run over him. The second group will be going toward the other basket: Players 2 and X2 will be attacking the other end of the court.
3. Players 1 and X1 pass the ball with sharp chest or bounce passes until 1 decides to drive to the basket with his dribble; 1 may decide to drive at any time, therefore X1 must be alert. Diagram 9-1 shows 1 driving after the sixth pass.
4. Player X1 must respond with good defensive denial of 1's attempt to dribble the ball into the middle lane; X1 must keep 1 under control.
5. Player X1 guards 1 until 1 scores, or X1 rebounds or steals.
6. Player 1 can change his direction or his pace at any moment while in the passing lane, but only when he does not have

the ball. This compels X1 to be ever alert. Defender X1 cannot hold the ball. As soon as X1 catches the ball, he must pass it.

7. Neither X1 nor 1 can walk with the ball. Each must pass upon receiving it until 1 decides to dribble drive.

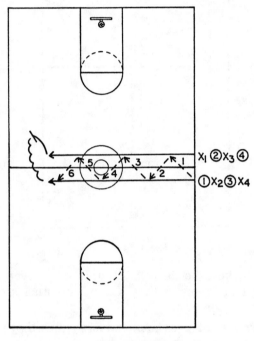

Diagram 9-1

Drill 146: Two-on-One Fast Break (7, 8, 9)

Objectives:

1. To teach X1 how to defend against two attackers when X1 is alone near the basket.
2. To teach two attackers how to always score in a two-on-one situation.
3. To teach the safety part of fast-break defense and the safety part of the full-court pressure defenses.

Procedure:

1. Line up players as shown in Diagram 9-2.
2. Rotate one offensive man to X1 after each attempt to score.

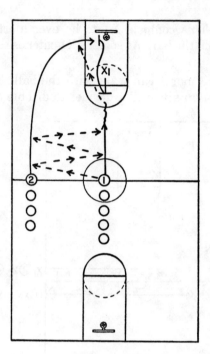

Diagram 9-2

The attacker who shoots or commits a turnover becomes the next X1 in defensive line; X1 and the other attacker go to the end of the line.

3. Players 1 and 2 pass back and forth until they near the top of the circle; 1 then tries to drive to the basket.

4. Defender X1 must stop 1; hopefully he will draw a charge.

5. If 1 passes off without charging X1, X1 must get back in time to stop 2, hopefully again drawing the charge.

6. You can extend the lines to three-quarter court or full-court.

7. You can have 1 spread out wider instead of coming down the middle of the court, simulating a wide two-lane fast break.

8. You could allow 2 to dribble drive to the basket while 1 comes down the middle lane for a pass and a lay-up.

Drill 147: Three-on-One Fast Break (7, 8, 9)

Objectives:

1. To teach one defender, X3, how to stop a three-on-one fast break.

2. To teach three attackers to develop a three-on-one attack.

3. To teach X3 to become an aggressive defender.

4. To teach drawing the charge.

5. To teach stopping one attacker yet recovering to another.

Procedure:

1. Line up players as shown in Diagram 9-3.

2. The player who shoots or turns the ball over stays on defense. The others rotate lines. To make sure all your potential starters play defense, you may have to make assignments instead of using the above rotation. You could, for example, make the lines rotate from 2 to 1 to X3 to 3 to 2.

3. Three players attack X3. They can do this with a dribble or a pass or a figure-eight passing weave.

4. Defender X3 tries to draw the charge on the dribbler, 1 in Diagram 9-3.

5. Should the dribbler pass off successfully, X3 must hurry back to stop the new receiver. Player X3 can try to block the shot by the new receiver, or X3 can attempt to draw the charge.

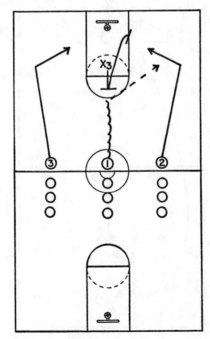

Diagram 9-3

Drill 148: Tandem Defense into Pressure Defense (7, 8, 9)

Objectives:

1. To teach X1 and X2 to play fast-break defense.
2. To teach instant conversion from defense to offense.
3. To teach shortstopping, denial, face-guarding, etc.
4. To teach run and jump and other defensive stunts.
5. To teach fast-break passing, cutting, and dribbling.
6. To condition defensively and offensively.

Procedure:

1. Line up players as shown in Diagram 9-4.
2. Rotate as illustrated below in sections 4, 5, and 6.
3. Players 1, 2, and 3 run a three-man figure-eight passing weave against X1 and X2; X1 and X2 are in a tandem defense (parallel, if you prefer).

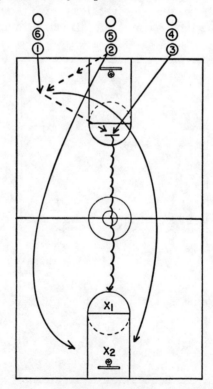

Diagram 9-4

4. Should X1 and X2 secure the ball because 3 scored on a jump shot, X1 and X2 would play a two-on-two full-court game against 1 and 2; 1 and 2 could face-guard, shortstop, run and jump, etc. Players 1 and 2 then hurry back down to become the next tandem defense for the attack from 4, 5, and 6.

5. If 3 missed the shot or throws the ball away, X1 and X2 fast break against 3 in a two-on-one situation. Players 1 and 2 become the next tandem defense.

6. If 2 scored, the two-on-two game would have X1 and X2 attacking 1 and 3. If 2 missed or threw the ball away, X1 and X2 would attack 2 in two-on-one fast-break situation.

7. You could have 1, 2, and 3 become full-court pressure defenders if 3 scores; X1 and X2 would in bounds the pass against shortstop or centerfield tactics. Repeated three-on-two run and jumps could be run (see Drill 126). Players 1 and 2 (because 3 scored) would race downfloor to play tandem defense when X1 or X2 shoots. Players 4, 5, and 6 would immediately begin their weave. This simulates actual game conditions.

Drill 149: Three-on-Three Call (7, 8, 9)

Objectives:

1. To teach retreating to a two-defender tandem. One must take the ball and let his teammate have the basket area. The one who takes the ball must let his teammate know he intends to cover the dribbler; he yells "ball." His teammate retreats to the area of the basket.

2. To teach the third defender that, by hustle, he can frequently get back to help the two defenders and make it a three-on-three situation.

3. To teach safety defense: three-on-two.

4. To teach a three-lane fast-break attack.

Procedure:

1. Place the entire team in three lines on the baseline. Three players are attackers (Diagram 9-5).

2. Take the front three out to the free throw line extended and have them face the three lines on the baseline. Each member at the free throw line extended should be paired with an attacker on the baseline. The three men at the free throw line extended are defenders.

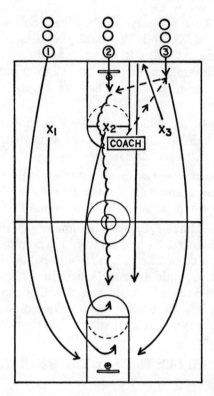

Diagram 9-5

3. Coach stands at the free throw line tossing the ball to one of the players on the baseline. The defender paired with that attacker must go touch the baseline before racing to the other end of the court to help on the three-on-two situation.

4. The three-on-two situation occurs because the three attackers fast break to the opposite end of the court while the remaining two defenders try to stop the fast-breaking attackers.

5. The coach goes to the other end and places the same three on defense and runs the drill back. The original attackers become defenders when they have attacked down the floor and back.

Drill 150: Three-on-Two-on-One (7, 8, 9)

Objectives:

1. To teach fast-break tandem defense.

2. To teach one defender how to stop a two-on-one fast break.

3. To teach a three-lane and two-lane fast break.

Procedure:

1. Line up players as shown in Diagram 9-6.

2. Players 1, 2, and 3 attack by using the figure-eight passing weave, by dribbling straight down the floor, or by passing as they go directly downcourt. Players 1, 2, and 3 attack X1 and X2.

3. Players X1 and X2 play a tandem defense (parallel, if you prefer). If X1 and X2 stop 1, 2, or 3, X1 and X2 will fast break against the shooter or the man who turned the ball over (two-on-one fast break). The other two attackers stay on defense as the next X1 and X2.

4. If 1, 2, or 3 score, X1 and X2 take the ball out and attack

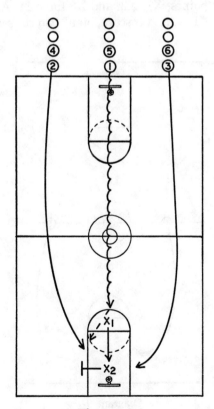

Diagram 9-6

two-on-one against the scorer. The other two attackers stay
as the next X1 and X2.

5. After the two-on-one attack, the new attackers and the defenders go to the end of the three lines. Players 4, 5, and 6
begin the next three-on-two-on-one.

Drill 151: Three-on-Three-on-Three-on-Three (7, 8, 9)

Objectives:

1. To teach tandem or parallel defense against the fast break.
2. To teach conversion from scoring into an immediate press.
3. To teach your defenders the slides you intend to use in your
   zone or man-to-man press.
4. To teach defenders that if they press well they can get back
   into a game when hopelessly down. Many times during the
   year, the score will be lopsided—for example, 1, 2, and 3
   have six points; X1, X2, and X3 have 11; A, B, and C have
   12. But if 1, 2, and 3 score, steal two consecutive inbounds

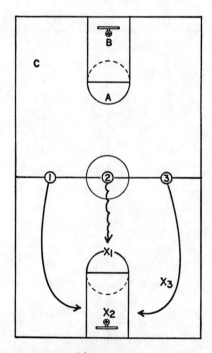

Diagram 9-7

passes, and score, they suddenly have nine. They're back in the game. It teaches a never-give-up attitude.

Procedure:

1. Players 1, 2, and 3 attack X1 and X2 (Diagram 9-7).
2. If X1 and X2 stop 1, 2, and 3, they outlet pass to X3, and then X1, X2, and X3 fast break against A, B, and C.
3. Should 1, 2, and 3 score, they immediately go to a full-court press. Player X1 or X2 takes the ball out, entering a pass to X3 or to X1 or X2 (whoever did not take the ball out).
4. Players 1, 2, and 3 can double-team, run and jump, or zone press. Players A, B, and C can come up as far as half court. To make it really difficult, you can let A, B, and C come to the 28-foot marker.
5. Should 1, 2, and 3 intercept, they fast break against X1, X2, and X3.
6. Should A, B, and C intercept, they fast break against X1, X2, and X3.
7. Keep score to fifteen baskets.
8. You can use teams of four if you like (1, 2, 3, 4) (X1, X2, X3, X4) (A, B, C, D) or you can use four teams of three. W, X, and Y would take the place of X1, X2, and X3 when they attack A, B, and C. Players 1, 2, and 3 drop off until W, X, and Y attack and the rotation continues.

Drill 152: Four Drill Offensively (7, 8, 9)

Objectives:

1. To condition.
2. To teach 1 the full-court driving lay-up.
3. To teach 2 to catch 1 before the lay-up.
4. To teach the proper offensive maneuvers for the three-on-one fast break.
5. To teach advancing the ball by passing.
6. To teach advancing the ball by dribbling.
7. To teach a lone defender to slow down the three-on-one break until help arrives, always being cognizant of preventing the lay-up.

8. To teach 3 how to defense against inbounds passing.
9. To teach 1 to free himself for an inbounds pass.

Procedure:

1. Line up your squad at the end of the floor as in the Three Drill Defensively (Drill 128) or the Four Drill Defensively (Drill 129).
2. Players 1, 2, and 3 perform the same feats on their down-floor trip as they did in the Three Drill Defensively (Drill 128) and the Four Drill Defensively (Drill 129).
3. Player 4 races downfloor to touch the baseline; he times his return trip to coincide with 2's inbounding the ball to 1.
4. Player 3 defends (denial, face-guard, etc.) against the pass to 1; 1 must receive the ball below the free throw line extended. Player 1 must maneuver to get open under pressure.
5. Once the ball is inbounded, it is a three-on-one fast break.

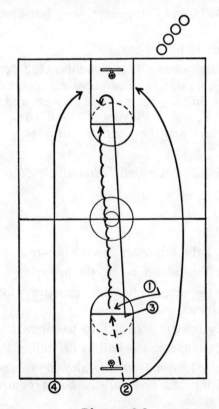

Diagram 9-8

6. Player 1 can take the center lane with 2 filling the outside lane, or 2 can take the center lane with 1 filling outside. This requires 1 and 2 to make a proper fast-break choice.

7. The dribbler, 1 in Diagram 9-8, brings the ball down the center lane. Players 2 and 4 fill the outside lanes, running about three feet inbounds until they reach the free throw line extended, then they make a 45 degree cut toward the basket. The cut is preceded by planting the outside foot and pushing hard for the basket. Players 2 and 4 can cross underneath or they can stop at the free throw line baseline. We prefer for 2 to stop. You can have 4 cross if you like.

8. Coach can require players to pass the ball, dribble, or combine the two as they run the length of the floor at full speed. Coach can have attackers weave (dribbling) the length of the floor or run the figure eight (passing). Use of all of these methods forces the attackers to think and to adjust instantly to different fast-break situation. Varying the routine will not only teach the players more fast-break basketball, but the variety will keep the drill fresh for the duration of the long basketball season.

Drill 153: Five Drill Offensively (7, 8, 9)

Objectives:

1. To condition.
2. To teach 2 to complete the inbounds pass against denial and face-guard pressure.
3. To teach 3 and 5 denial and face-guard techniques.
4. To teach 2, 1, and 4 how to fast break against two defenders.
5. To teach 3 and 5 the tandem or safety defense.
6. To teach 3 and 5 to fast break immediately after stealing an errant pass.

Procedure:

1. Line up players as shown in Diagram 9-9, which is the same as the Four Drill Offensively (Drill 152).
2. Players 1, 2, 3, and 4 perform the same functions when they first race downfloor as they did in the Four Drill Offensively (Drill 152).
3. After the trip downfloor, 5 covers 4, trying to prevent the inbounds pass. His defense may be face-guard, denial, etc.

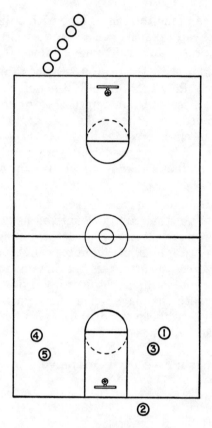

Diagram 9-9

If it is face-guard or denial, 4 must receive the ball below the free throw line extended.

4. In the early stages of the drill, before all concerned become proficient at their skills, 1 and 4 cannot cross against face-guard pressure. After 2, 3, and 5 learn the proper offensive and defensive face-guarding tactics and become adept at the execution of them, 1 and 4 not only can cross, but they can line up in a tandem or any other method of attack they choose or the coach directs. It is good to practice the offensive methods employed by the next opposition.

5. Once 2 passes inbounds to either 1 or 4, they fast break against 3 and 5. Coaches can require the three attackers to pass the ball only, to dribble only, or to combine the two.

6. Players 3 and 5 can play pressure defense after the ball is

passed inbounds, or they can race back to defend in a tandem near their goal.

7. Should 3 or 5 intercept any pass, they fast break against 1, 2, and 4.

8. The guard who receives the inbounds pass should fill the center lane while 2 and the other guard fill the outside lanes.

Drill 154: Six Drill Offensively (7, 8, 9)

Objectives:

1. To condition.

2. To teach the four-on-two, the three-on-two, and two-on-one fast-break offensive and defensive situations.

3. To force players to adjust constantly when recovering a loose ball or a rebound.

4. To teach 3 and 5 pressure defenses and how to retreat to a tandem or parallel fast-break or safety defense.

Procedure:

1. Line up all players except two at the end line as in the Five Drill Offensively. Line up these two in the corners on the opposite end line (X1 and X2 in Diagram 9-10).

2. On their trip downfloor, 1, 2, 3, 4, and 5 perform as they did in the Five Drill Offensively (Drill 153).

3. Player 6 races downfloor and assumes a position out-of-bounds in either the outside lanes or the middle lane; 6 has the choice. Different positioning by 6 aids all players in learning to adjust to defensive coverage.

4. After the trip downfloor, 2 passes into either 1 or 4. After the ball is passed inbounds, 2 and 6 must decide on the lanes they are to fill and the drill becomes a four-on-two fast break.

5. If 1, 2, 4, and 6 do not get the immediate lay-up or the easy jump shot on the return trip, they activate the next group into the Six Drill Offensively.

6. Players 3 and 5 run a tandem defense against the four-man assault; or 3 and 5 play a parallel defense.

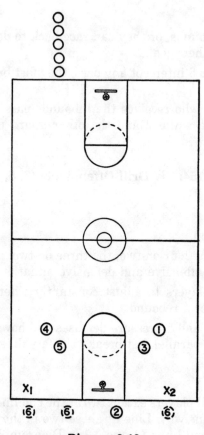

Diagram 9-10

7. After 1, 2, 4, and 6 score or 3 and 5 intercept, the two defenders, 3 and 5, along with the trailer (whoever shoots or throws the ball away among 1, 2, 4, and 6) attack X1 and X2 in a three-on-two fast-break situation.

8. When X1 and X2 stop the three-man break or when the three attackers score, X1 and X2 attack the middle-lane man in a two-on-one fast-break situation.

9. The two outside men in the three-on-two fast break stay downfloor becoming the next X1 and X2.

10. A new 6 begins another wave of action as the two-on-one break reaches midcourt.

10

Combination
of Maneuvers
Defensive Drills

Successful seasons and careers depend upon the creativeness of the coach. The coach must consistently "create" drills to correct the faults of his team. Sometimes these faults are fundamental and therefore individual in nature. But all too often they involve the ability to move from one fundamental to another fundamental and yet stay within the framework set forth in executing the coach's adopted defense for that season; court savvy is a better description of it. To drill on these faults, a coach must offer multipurpose or multitraining drills.

Single-purpose defensive fundamental drills teach what to do, how to do it, and why the defender must do it. To teach the all-important "when to do it" requires a multipurpose drill.

When a player is not performing one particular fundamental well, the coach can still elect to use a multidimensional drill; you would need merely to emphasize that one poorly executed fundamental. This emphasis quickly corrects the execution of that one fundamental, and the savvy gained from the multipurpose drilling will not be lost. This is especially important for late-season drilling, long after individual fundamentals should have been mastered.

Within this chapter 18 multidimensional drills are offered, covering many types of situations. If you cannot find a drill that covers your needs, perhaps one is close enough that it can be an acceptable substitute, or, even better, perhaps the "almost perfect" drill will inspire you to "create" the exact one you want. Happy hunting. Think and create well. Your next game, your career maybe, depends upon it. More important, there is a squad of young and very eager faces depending on *you*.

Drill 155: Baseline Close-Out and Approach Drill (3, 4, 5)

Objectives:

1. To teach defenders how to approach an attacker without allowing the attacker an advantage.
2. To teach defenders how to close out baseline drives yet maintain excellent positioning on inside drives.
3. To teach good one-on-one offense and defense.

Procedure:

1. Line up players as shown in Diagram 10-1.
2. Rotate from offense to defense to end of the line. First player in line becomes the next attacker.
3. Player X1 rolls the ball to 1; 1 fakes and drives.
4. Defender X1 must close the baseline drive yet maintain excellent defensive positioning on inside drives.

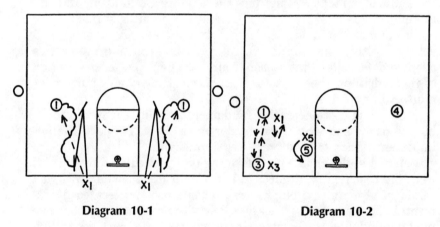

Diagram 10-1   Diagram 10-2

Drill 156: Dive-and-Rotate Drill (3, 4, 5, 6)

Objectives:

1. To teach X1 and X3 how to sag one and one-half steps toward each pass.
2. To teach X5 how to defense the low post.
3. To teach X1 and X3 when and how to dive inside and help X5 on a successful pass completion into the low-post player, X5 in Diagrams 10-2 and 10-3.

4. To teach X5, the weakside deep defender, to "rotate" onto the breakaway dribbler, 4 in Diagram 10-3 (see Drill 55).

5. To teach X1 to drop and cover the post area (The Rotation Drill, Drill 55).

6. To teach X5 to draw the charge on the driving 4.

7. To teach X5 to defend the low-post attacker who has the ball.

8. To teach 5 how to attack quickly one-on-one inside.

9. To teach good perimeter and inside passing.

Procedure:

1. Line up players as shown in Diagrams 10-2 and 10-3.

2. Rotate from 1 to X1 to 3 to X3 to 5 to X5 to 4 to end of the line. First player in line becomes the new 1.

3. Player X3 must not be permitted to defend 3 in the beginning.

4. Players 1 and 3 pass the ball looking to get the ball inside to 5. Should 5 get the ball, he immediately goes one-on-one against X5; X1 and X3 should be trying to keep X5 from getting the ball. Player X1 or X3, whoever is responsible for the dive in your defensive schemes, should immediately help X5 when 5 receives the pass.

5. After a few successful passes inside to 5, either 1 or 3 pass to 4 (Diagram 10-3). Player 4, upon receiving the pass, drives hard to the basket. Defender X5 must come over to stop 4's drive; X5 then yells "rotate," activating the Rotation Drill (Drill 55). Player X1, upon hearing "rotate," drops down to cover 5.

Drill 157: Screen on or Away, or Cut (3, 4, 5)

Objectives:

1. To teach defenders how to play screens on the ball (your rules) and screens away from the ball (your rules).

2. To teach defenders how to cover the middle cut, the give and go, and the backdoor cuts.

3. To teach the attackers to screen away, to screen on the ball, to middle cut, to give and go, and to backdoor cut.

4. To teach defenders to close the gap defensively.

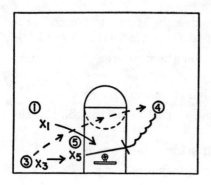

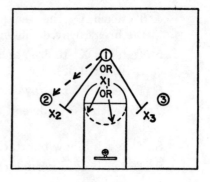

Diagram 10-3   Diagram 10-4

Procedure:

1. Line up players as shown in Diagram 10-4.
2. Rotate from offense to defense to end of the line. First three players in line become the new offense.
3. Player 1 may pass to 2 or to 3. He goes to screen on the ball or away. He may elect to cut backdoor, middle, or give and go. Players 2 or 3 can try to free themselves by cutting backdoor.
4. You can require in the beginning that players only screen on or only screen away, or you can only allow cutting. This makes the drill more specific and not really multipurpose.
5. You can allow dribbling after screening and cutting have been mastered. This would require defenders to close the gap.
6. You can combine all the action (dribbling, cutting, and screening), requiring the three defenders to read and to react.

Drill 158: Covering Cutting Maneuvers (3)

Objectives:

1. To teach defense of give-and-go (cutting between defender and ball) and backdoor (cutting behind the defender) cutters.
2. To teach backdoor and give-and-go cutting maneuvers.
3. To teach defensive concentration.
4. To teach passes on give-and-go and backdoor cuts.
5. To teach driving after receiving a pass on a cut.

6. To teach driving for a lay-up under extreme defensive pressure.
7. To teach proper defense on lay-up attempts.

Procedure:

1. Line up players as shown in Diagram 10-5. Rotate from offense to defense to end of the line.
2. Coach passes ball to one offensive man; the other offensive man cuts anywhere except behind the man with the ball—a give-and-go, middle, or backdoor cut.
3. The offense keeps passing the ball until they get a driving lay-up either as a give-and-go, middle, or backdoor cut. If any defensive man allows the give-and-go cut, it must be corrected immediately.
4. No dribbling is allowed except upon receiving a pass as a cutter; then the dribble may be used while driving to the basket.

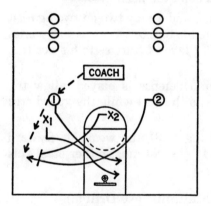

Diagram 10-5   Diagram 10-6

Drill 159: Forward-Forward Denial (3, 4, 5)

Objectives:

1. To teach denial of the penetrating pass.
2. To teach denial of the flash pivot (X4 keeping 4 from receiving the pass).
3. To teach defense of cutting maneuvers.
4. To teach proper corner defense by X3 and X4.
5. To teach offensive corner moves by 3 and 4.

6. To teach zoning principles (also a man principle).

7. To teach pressure stances and movements.

Procedure:

1. Players 1 and 2 pass inside to 3 or 4; X3 and X4 try to deny 3 and 4 the ball. Rotate from offense to defense to end of the line. The guards who pass the ball become the next defenders. The first man in line becomes the next guard.

2. Begin by letting 1 and 2 pass the ball back and forth. Each holds the ball for a two count. When 1 has the ball, X3 denies 3. When 2 has the ball, X4 denies 4 the ball. When 1 has the ball, X4 sags; and when 2 has the ball, X3 sags.

3. Players 1 and 2 are not allowed to move. Neither is the opposite forward. This makes X3 and X4 hustle to maintain proper positioning (Diagram 10-6).

4. Start the drill by letting 1 pass to 3; X3 pressures 3.

5. Player X4 must get set to deny the flash pivot.

6. When 4 receives the pass, 3 and 4 play two-on-two against X3 and X4. Should 4 be unable to receive the pass, 3 passes back to 1 who passes to 2. Player 4 hurries to his position while X4 tries to deny.

7. You can, after great denial defense is played, allow the weakside forward to flash to the ball while the guard still has the ball.

8. On backdoor cuts (1 passing to 3), the weakside forward (X4) must stop the play. Player X4 must either steal this pass or draw the charge.

Drill 160: Three-Man Multipurpose Drill (3)

Objectives:

1. To teach inside defense.

2. To teach defense of the screen and roll.

3. To teach defense of the backdoor.

4. To teach defense of the flash pivot.

5. To teach defense of a driver.

6. To teach the proper rotation of an escaped dribbler.

7. To teach offensive fakes and drives.

8. To teach backdoor passing, inside passing, and perimeter passing under maximum defensive pressure.

Procedure:

1. Line up players as shown in Diagrams 10-7 and 10-8.

2. Rotate from offense to defense to end of the line. The first three men in the line become the new offensive players.

3. Player 1 starts with the ball. Player 2 goes and screens for 3; 2 rolls across the lane. If 1 cannot hit 3, 3 can go backdoor. This type screening and rolling continues until the offense scores or the defense steals the ball or rebounds a missed shot.

4. You can make the drill tougher by not allowing 1, 2, or 3 to dribble. This greatly improves passing and pressuring.

5. You can require only lay-ups. This forces real defensive teamwork.

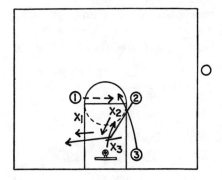

Diagram 10-7

Diagram 10-8

Drill 161: Three-on-Three Guard-Forward Combination Drill (3)

Objectives:

1. To teach X1 and X2 proper defensive guard techniques.

2. To teach X3 proper defensive techniques on defending the corner and post men.

3. To teach good one-on-one defensive and offensive play.

4. To teach the defenders how to defend a combination of areas in one drill: in this case, from the strongside corner to side pivot to flash pivot to weakside corner.

5. To teach proper perimeter defensive and offensive techniques.

6. To teach 3 how to get open against pressure and denial defense.

Procedure:

1. Line up players on the side of the court as shown in Diagram 10-9.
2. Rotate from 1 to X1 to 2 to X2 to 3 to X3 to end of the line. First player in line becomes the new 1.
3. Player 1 passes to 2 while X1 and X2 step in and toward every pass. Player X3 must constantly readjust his positioning.
4. Players 3 and X3 play corner offense and defense into pivot offense and defense into opposite-corner offense and defense.
5. If 1 or 2 can pass the ball into 3, they do. Should the pass be completed, you can either allow 3 and X3 to play one-on-one while X1 and X2 dive and help or you can allow all players to play three-on-three.

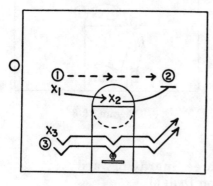

Diagram 10-9

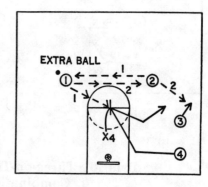

Diagram 10-10

Drill 162: Deny Flash Pivot—Contest Pass (3)

Objectives:

1. To condition defensively.
2. To teach proper defensive flash-pivot techniques.
3. To teach inside defensive men to get the advantage by hustling.
4. To teach it is never too late to recover to a contesting defensive position.

5. To teach deflection of a pass, yet recovery to another attacker.

6. To teach offensive and defensive one-on-one play.

7. To teach good passing and cutting techniques offensively.

Procedure:

1. Line up players as shown in Diagram 10-10. Have two balls available for use.

2. Rotate from 3 to 4 to 1 to 2 to X4 to end of the line. First player in line becomes the next 3.

3. Player 2 has the ball first and will pass to 1; 1 has the extra ball at his feet.

4. Player 4 tries to break into the flash-pivot area and X4 beats him to the most advantageous spot.

5. Player 1 throws a pass to 4 but X4 must deflect it. If the pass is completed, X4 and 4 go one-on-one.

6. After Step 4 is completed, 1 passes the extra ball to 2 who passes to 3. Player X4 tries to contest the pass to 3. Should 3 receive the pass, 3 and X4 go one-on-one.

Drill 163: Continuous-Movement Drill (3)

Objectives:

1. To teach defense to be alert and to use aggressive footwork.

2. To teach avoiding the screen by opening up and sliding through.

3. To teach defense of a quick popping-out attacker.

4. To teach defense of the driver.

5. To teach proper rotation by activating the rotation drill.

6. To teach defense of the backdoor cut.

7. To teach offense to be constantly in motion.

Procedure:

1. Line up players as shown in Diagrams 10-11 and 10-12 (four against four).

2. Rotate from offense to defense to end of the line. First four in line become the new offense.

3. Player 1 screens down and 3 pops out (Diagram 10-11). Player 2 passes to 3; 2 screens down for 4 and 4 pops out.

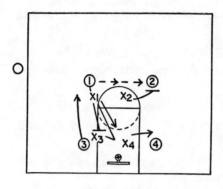 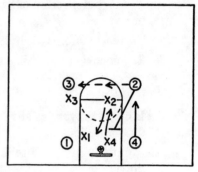

Diagram 10-11   Diagram 10-12

Player 3 drives when he first receives the pass. If 2 cannot pass to 3, 3 goes backdoor and/or screens down for 1.

4. All defenders stay with their own assignments. Player X1 in Diagram 10-11 opens up and allows X3 to slide through. This allows X3 to deny 3 the pass, possibly intercepting it.

5. When 2 passes to 3, he goes to screen for 4. Player X2 opens up and allows X4 to slide through.

6. You can also allow the baseline players to screen across for each other.

7. This screening and backdoor cutting permits the drill to be continuous. You can spread the offense using the half-court or you can compact it to the area around the free throw lane.

Drill 164: Screen on Ball and Roll and Pop Out (3)

Objectives:

1. To teach defending against screening on the ball and the roll that follows.

2. To defense the pop-out offensive maneuver.

3. To teach weakside assistance on the roll to the basket.

4. To teach the offense to screen and roll.

5. To teach the offense to screen down on the weakside.

6. To teach offense to pop out for a jump shot.

Procedure:

1. Line up four players against four as shown in Diagram 10-13.

2. Rotate from offense to defense to next group of positions: from offense to defense and from 3 to 5 and X3 to X5; from offense to defense and from 2 to 4 and X2 to X4.

3. Coach passes to either 2 or to 3. He passes to 3 in Diagram 10-13.

4. Immediately, 3 drives off 5's screen. Player 5 can screen on either side.

5. Defenders X5 and X3 jump switch. On the weak side, 2 screens for 4. Defenders X2 and X4 stay with their assignments; X4 slides through. Player X2 helps on 5's roll to the basket.

6. Player 3 can hit 4 for a jump shot, 3 can hit 2 on a pinning move for a lay-up, or 3 can hit 5 for a lay-up as 5 rolls. Player 3 can drive for a lay-up or stop and shoot the jump shot.

7. If none of the above work, 3 passes to the coach and the drill begins again.

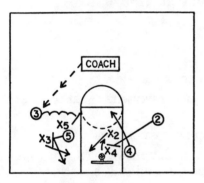

Diagram 10-13

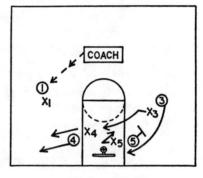

Diagram 10-14

Drill 165: Defense of Shuffle Cut, Give and Go, and Posting (3)

Objectives:

1. To teach defenders how to cover the shuffle cut, the give and go, and a post up.

2. To teach attackers how to dip to set up the shuffle cut.

3. To teach screening involved in shuffle cut.

Procedure:

1. Line up players four against four as shown in Diagram 10-14.

2. Rotate from offense to defense to next group of positions: from offense to defense and from 1 to 4 and X1 to X4; from offense to defense and from 3 to 5 and X3 to X5.

3. Coach passes either to 1 or to 3. He passes to 1 in Diagram 10-14.

4. Immediately, 3 sets up X3 to rub X3 off on 5.

5. Defender X3 goes over the top of the screen set by 5. Player X5 sags and helps on the cut before recovering on his own man; X5 could step in front of 3 and draw the charge if that defensive play develops.

6. Player 4, meanwhile, broke to the corner. If 1 cannot pass to the cutting 3, he passes to 4. When 1 passes to 4, 1 cuts through on the give and go. Player 4 dribbles outside looking to pass to the posting 3; 1 cuts through to the weakside.

7. Player 4 passes to the coach, and the drill begins again.

Drill 166: Strongside Drill with Trap (3, 4, 5)

Objectives:

1. To teach strongside defensive play.

2. To teach X1 to stop 1's drive to the outside.

3. To teach X2 to recognize when a reverse is about to occur and to go trap.

4. To teach X3 to shoot the gap for possible steals.

5. To teach defensive recovery and not allow a shot when the offense passes successfully out of a difficult situation.

6. To teach proper rotation.

Procedure:

1. Line up players as shown in Diagram 10-15.

2. Rotate from 1 to 2 to 3 to X3 to X2 to X1 to end of the line. First player in line becomes the next 1.

3. Player 1 is the only player who can drive to the weakside. This keeps the defense honest. When 1 drives to the weakside, X1 must cut him off and X2 must anticipate the cutoff. At the exact moment of the reverse by 1, X2 goes to trap.

4. Should 1 drive by X1, X2 and X3 become weakside defenders. Player X3 must stop the breakaway dribbler (Drill 55) and X2 must rotate down on 3; X3 calls "rotate."

5. Players 1, 2, and 3 can do any move on the strongside. For example, 2 could screen down for 3. Players X1, X2, and X3 must use proper strongside defensive techniques (whatever your defensive rules are for the coverages used by 1, 2, and 3's offensive maneuvers.

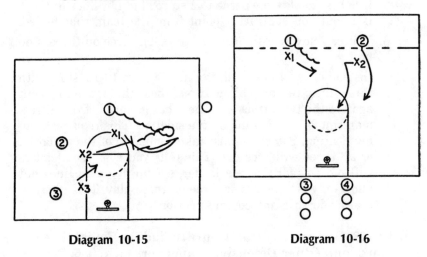

Diagram 10-15   Diagram 10-16

Drill 167: Two-on-Two-on-Two-on-Two (3, 4, 5)

Objectives:

1. To teach defensive alertness.
2. To teach the entire spectrum of defensive skills.
3. To teach defensive hustle.
4. To teach the enjoyment of playing defense.
5. To teach offensive attack quickness.
6. To teach defensive communication.

Procedure:

1. Line up players as shown in Diagram 10-16.
2. Players 1 and 2 attack X1 and X2, using whatever offensive maneuver they think may work. Defenders X1 and X2 use their defensive tactics to counter 1 and 2.
3. If 1 or 2 score, they must advance the ball beyond the dotted line then attack again. Players 3 and 4 become the new defensive men. Players X1 and X2 go to the end of the line.

4. If X1 and X2 stop 1 and 2, X1 and X2 must advance the ball beyond the dotted line; then they attack. Players 3 and 4 become the new defensive men, while 1 and 2 go to the end of the line.

5. It is best to play the game to a score of ten by ones. If there is a foul you subtract a point from the team that fouled.

6. You can advance the drill to three-on-three-on-three, and up.

7. Instead of two lines as shown in Diagram 10-16, start with three lines. But only allow two of these three men to go out against the two attackers. The other member of this three-man squad would stand on the sideline. This requires communication. Someone must take command of the situation or all three will race out. This tells you who your leaders will be. To really find a leader, set up five-man lines but allow only two-on-two or three-on-three play. This requires real leadership and communication.

Drill 168: One-on-One Half Court Including Denial, Face-Guard, and Other Defensive Maneuvers (3, 4, 5, 6, 7, 8)

Objectives:

1. To teach individual one-on-one defense.
2. To teach individual one-on-one offensive moves.
3. To teach transition from offense to defense.
4. To teach blocking out.
5. To teach offensive rebounding.
6. To teach denial of the outlet pass.
7. To teach the outlet pass.
8. To teach inbounding the pass against denial pressure.

Procedure:

1. Line up three players at each basket. Player X2 attacks X1.
2. If X2 scores, X1 takes the ball out-of-bounds and passes to X3. Player X2 defends X3 with denial, face-guard, etc. If X3 receives the pass inbounds, X2 must immediately keep X3 from scoring (Diagram 10-17).
3. If X2 misses, X1 blocks off the boards, rebounds, and hits X3 with an outlet pass, simulating a fast break. Player X2 turns and defends X3.

4. After getting the ball to X3, X1 goes to the end of the line and the drill continues. You can keep score to a certain number of points, or you can let the winner be the player who scores three consecutive times.

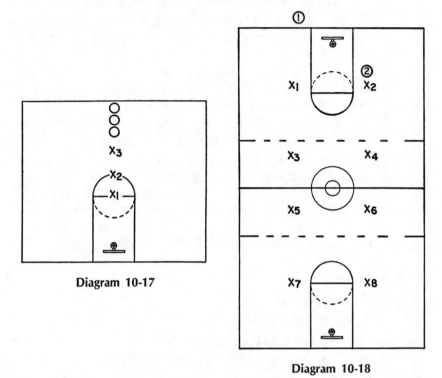

Diagram 10-17

Diagram 10-18

Drill 169: Full-Court Denial, Shortstop into Two-on-Two Half Court (3, 4, 5, 6, 7, 8, 9)

Objectives:

1. To teach inbounds denial techniques.

2. To teach run and jump (require 1 and 2 to dribble), to teach trapping (X1 and X2, for example, trap 2), to teach shooting the gap for steals, and to teach stopping the breakaway dribbler.

3. To teach the slides of your zone press.

4. To teach half-court offense and defense.

5. To teach safety, tandem, and parallel defenses of the transition game.

Procedure:

1. Two offensive players attack eight defenders (Diagram 10-18).
2. Defenders can only cover areas inside their dotted lines.
3. Players 1 and 2 can be required to pass instead of dribbling, you can require dribbling, or you can require a mixture of the two.
4. Players X1 and X2 can double-team 2, shortstop 2, pressure 1 and deny 2, etc. This takes in all the possible defensive pressure techniques you want to employ.
5. Players X3 and X4 deny passes into their area. They can also trap, but they must stop the breakaway dribbler.
6. Whenever attackers pass up a defensive area, those defenders drop off to the side of the court. When 1 and 2 score against X7 and X8, they bring the ball back. Should any defender intercept, he and his teammate fast break.

Drill 170: Two-on-Two-on-Two Full Court (3, 4, 5, 6, 7, 8, 9)

Objectives:

1. To teach defenders to full-court press.
2. To condition defensively.
3. To teach run-and-jump stunts.
4. To teach shortstop and centerfield tactics.
5. To teach offensive players to handle the basketball against great pressure.

Procedure:

1. Line up players as shown in Diagram 10-19.
2. To begin the drill, you pair off members of the team into groups of two.
3. Players 1 and 2 attack X1 and X2.
4. If 1 and 2 score, X1 and X2 go to the end of the line behind 5 and 6. Players 3 and 4 throw the ball in and 1 and 2 defend against 3 and 4 over the full court.
5. If 1 and 2 miss the shot or commit a turnover, X1 and X2 attack 1 and 2. If X1 and X2 score on their attack, 1 and 2 go to the end of the line behind C and D. Players A and B throw

the ball in bounds and X1 and X2 defend against A and B over the full court.

6. The drill continues in this fashion until a group of two score three consecutive baskets.

7. You could keep score to 10, 12, or 15. The first team reaching 10, 12, or 15 wins and receives an award.

8. On any foul, you subtract a point from that two-man team's score.

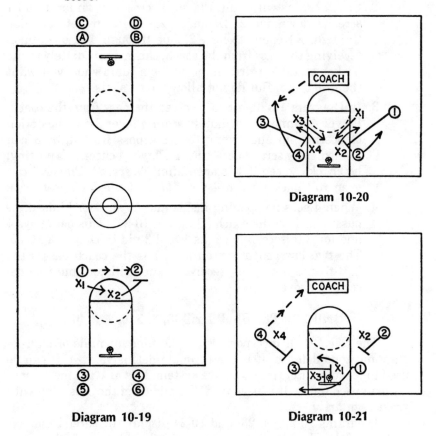

Diagram 10-20

Diagram 10-19

Diagram 10-21

Drill 171: Screen Down—Screen Across (3)

Objectives:

1. To teach defenders to open up and let their teammates slide through on downscreens.

2. To teach defense of the screen across the baseline low-post positions.

3. To teach defense of the passing game.

4. To teach one-on-one offensive and defensive play.

Procedure:

1. Line up players as shown in Diagrams 10-20 and 10-21.

2. Coach begins with ball. Player 3 screens down for 4 and 1 screens down for 2. Defender X3 opens to let X4 slide through; X1 opens to let X2 slide through. If 2 or 4, upon receiving the pass from the coach, can go immediately to the basket or take a dribble or so for a jump shot, you want them to do so. But do not allow forced shots.

3. In Diagram 10-20, 4 has received the pass from the coach. Player 4 cannot immediately score. Player 3 has the option of posting up and trying to get a pass from 4, or 3 can immediately screen across for 1. Player 4 checks 3's posting; he checks to see if 1 is open after 3's screen. Player 3 can even roll back toward 4 for a pass at the high-post area.

4. When 4 sees no opening inside and no shot for himself, he passes back to the coach (Diagram 10-21). This pass keys 4 and for 2 to screen down as 1 and 3 did in Diagram 10-20. The two low people screen across as the coach passes the ball to the new wing receivers; the drill continues as described above.

Drill 172: The Shell Drill (3, 4, 5, 6, 7, 8, 9)

The *Shell* Drill incorporates all the fundamentals of man-to-man and zone defense. It is the ultimate defensive drill. It can be used to teach your entire defensive system. It is also the most popular drill used today. It is used from the middle of the season on with great regularity.

Diagrams 10-22, 10-23, and 10-24 display the three basic formations of the Shell Drill. Diagram 10-22 should be used when your next opponent runs a two-guard-front offensive formation (2-1-2, 2-2-1, etc). We will use this diagram to discuss all the phases of the Shell Drill. You can convert each drill to the other formations. Diagram 10-23 exhibits the perfect Shell for the opponents whose offensive formation resembles a 1-3-1. Diagram 10-24 easily represents all formations that use a double stack or the very popular 1-2-2 formation.

Shell Game from the 2-2 Positioning

Procedure:

1. Line up players as shown in Diagram 10-22.
2. Rotate from 1 and 2 to X1 and X2, from 3 and 4 to X3 and X4. Then put 1, 2, X1, and X2 on the back line and 3, 4, X3, and X4 on the front or guard positions. Then bring on the next eight players.
3. Because this diagram is used to explain the entire Shell Drill, each phase will be fully explained as we discuss that segment of the Shell Drill in the following pages.

Shell Game from the 1-2-1 Positioning

Procedure:

1. Line up players as shown on the side of the court in Diagram 10-23.

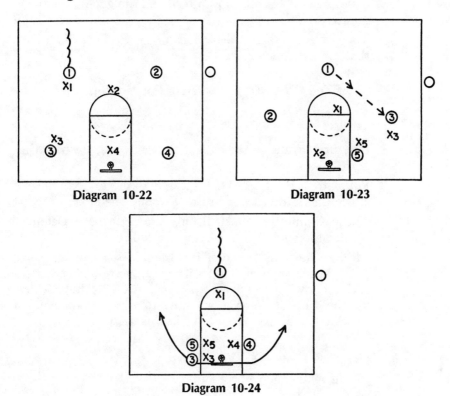

Diagram 10-22   Diagram 10-23

Diagram 10-24

2. Rotate from 3 to X3 to 1 to X1 to 2 to X2 to 5 to X5 to the end of the line. First player in line becomes the new 3.

3. At the beginning, we allow only 5 to move offensively. The other offensive players drill on passing, and the defenders drill on the use of the sag-in-and-toward-every-pass principle (both man-to-man and zone).

4. Limit 5's movement to high-, side-, and low-pivot positions. After you learn defense of the flash pivot, 5 is permitted to cut through the lane. Later you can allow 2 and 3 to screen down for 5, exchanging positions with him.

5. Player X5 must cover 5 correctly. Defenders X1, X2, and X3 cover their men with correct defensive outside techniques.

6. Once the ball is passed into 5, he goes one-on-one with either X1, X2, or X3 sinking to force the ball back out (Dive Drill).

7. After proper inside defense is learned, you can begin to allow 1, 2, or 3 to drive. This requires X1, X2, and X3 to close the gap and X5 to rotate should the gap-closing technique fail.

8. You can activate all the other maneuvers of the Shell Drill that are discussed later.

Shell Game from the 1-1-2 Positioning

Procedure:

1. Line up players on the side of the court as shown in Diagram 10-24.

2. Rotate from 1 to X1 to 3 to X3 to 4 to X4 to 5 to X5 to the end of the line. First player in line becomes the next 1.

3. At the beginning of the drill, only allow 3 to move. Defender X3 must keep 3 from receiving the ball.

4. After X3 has mastered denial of the pass to the wing, we go to the inside move of 4 and 5. They can post up or screen for each other with a roll back to the ball. After X4 and X5 have mastered inside defense, we move to all the maneuvers of the Shell Drill explained later in this section.

Objectives of the entire Shell Drill:

1. To teach defensive positioning.

2. To teach closing the gap.

3. To teach driving by offense, passing inside by the offense, and the dive by defenders to help out on passes into the post.
4. To teach denial of the flash pivot.
5. To teach defense of cutters.
6. To teach defense of the screen-away offensive strategy.
7. To teach defense of the screen-on-the-ball offensive attack.
8. To teach defensive rotations.
9. To teach post defense.
10. To teach your defensive stunts.
11. To teach help and recover.
12. To teach contesting the penetrating pass.
13. To deny the backdoor cut.
14. To teach defense of the lob pass.

Procedure of All Parts of the Shell Drill:

Because of the multiple nature of the Shell Drill and its all-encompassing aspects, we will divide the drill into twelve parts, explaining each as though it were an entity within itself. Line up all players in the formation of your next opponent, putting your defenders on the men you intend to be their assignments. We will use Diagram 10-22 to explain each separate part of the Shell Drill. Be sure X1 and X2 also get to play X3 and X4's positions and vice versa if you intend to teach man-to-man defense.

I. <u>Positioning</u>:

1. Players 1, 2, 3, and 4 pass the ball around using skip passes if you wish. They hold the ball three seconds after each pass reception.
2. Players X1, X2, X3, and X4 adjust their defensive positioning as each pass is in flight.
3. After each pass, the coach checks the defensive positioning of each player, correcting those who are out of position.

II. <u>Closing the Gap</u>:

1. Players 1, 2, 3, and 4 drive. If they cannot go all the way to the basket, they pass to a teammate.
2. Players X1, X2, X3, and X4 must help on the drive, then recover to their own assignment.

3. Let's let 1 drive to the left of X1 (Diagram 10-22). Player X3 must stop the drive. When 1 passes to 3, X3 must recover.

4. Each attacker takes turns driving and passing off until all holes have been driven into several times.

III. Pass Penetration:

1. On all the drills of the Shell Game, whenever a pass is completed into a side, the high, or the low post, those defenders responsible for diving and forcing the pass back out must be made aware of their duties; any mistakes must be immediately corrected.

IV. Flash-Pivot Defense:

1. Player 1 passes to 3. Player 4 flashes toward the ball. Player X3 would contest the pass from 1 to 3.

2. Player X4 denies the flash to 4.

3. Player X2 sags and helps; so does X1.

4. Player X3 pressures 3. If 3 completes the pass to 4, you can allow the players to perform a certain offensive maneuver (like split the post) or you can allow free-lance cutting while 4 goes one-on-one against X4. Players X1 and X2 should dive and force the ball back out.

5. If 3 cannot complete the pass to 4, he passes to 1 who passes to 2. While this passing is occuring, 4 moves from the flash pivot back to his original position. Player 2 hits 4 when 4 can free himself, and 3 flashes to the ball. Player X3 denies this flash pivot, and the drill continues until 3 or 4 receive the pass.

V. Cutter Drill:

1. Whenever 1 passes to 2 or to 3, 1 cuts through the lane.

2. Player X1 must jump in the direction of the pass by 1 or 1 gains a cutting advantage; X1 must maintain ballside defense on 1 during the entire cut.

3. Player 1 can cut out on 3's side or on 4's side.

4. Player 1 can post up so X1 must know how to cover the low post.

5. Player 1 was used to describe the drill, but 2, 3, or 4 can cut after they pass.

6. You can then advance the drill by allowing anyone to cut regardless of whether they passed the ball or not.

VI. Screen Away:

1. Player 1 passes to 3 and screens 2's defender; 2 uses the screen to cut to the basket. If 1 had wished, he could have screened 4's man instead of 2's.

2. If 1 had passed to 2, 1 could have screened for 3.

3. Player X1, according to our rules, opens up and allows the defender being screened to slide between defender X1 and the screener unless the cut occurs in scoring position. In that case, we fight over the top of the screener. You should use your rule.

4. You can advance the drill by allowing any player to set the screen regardless of whether he was the passer or not. This sometimes leads to free-lance multiple screens, so you must have already taught your rule for defensing multiple screens.

VII. Screen on the Ball:

1. When 1 passes to 3, he screens 3's defender. When 3 uses 1's screen, 1 will roll to the basket for a pass back.

2. Player 1 could pass to 2 and go screen and roll, or any attacker can follow his pass with a screen and a roll.

3. Our defensive rule on screens on the ball: We aggressively jump switch and have the weakside defenders help defense the roll to the basket.

4. We have, on occasions, trapped the screen on the ball and played the passing lanes. You want to use your defensive rule.

VIII. Rotations:

1. As either 1 or 3 drives to the basket (Diagrams 10-25 and 10-26), the weakside deep defender, X4, must stop the driver. Our weakside guard or wing drops to defend the basket. The defender on the ball rotates to the weakside guard or wing.

2. You can allow drives at anytime by any player with the ball. When that player breaks free of his own man, you must activate the rotation part of the Shell Drill (see Drill 55).

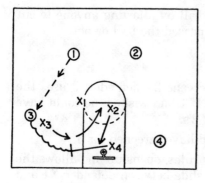

Diagram 10-25

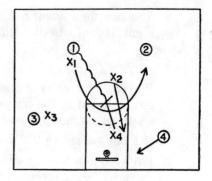

Diagram 10-26

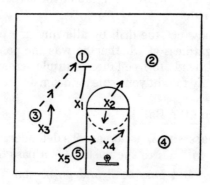

Diagram 10-27

IX. Shell Drill with a Post:

1. You can run your Shell Drill by activating only parts of the Shell Drill and activate a post man. For example, you might only want passing, teaching X1, X2, X3, and X4 proper defensive positioning. Yet you allow your post freedom of play (Diagram 10-27).

2. You might allow only lob passing into the post and no perimeter moves.

3. You might allow only lob passing into the post but passing and cutting by the perimeter. Your imagination is the only limit to your use of the Shell Drill with a post man. Remember: Any completed pass inside to the post man should activate the Dive Drill.

X. Activating Several Parts of the Shell Drill:

1. You could allow simultaneous screening on and away from the ball. Your defender must be alert as to the defense they wish to employ.

2. You could rule: Cutting on all vertical passes but screening on all horizontal ones.

3. You could demand dribbling penetration (Closing-the-Gap Drill) and yet allow flash pivoting away from the ball-side.

4. You could activate Step 3 above with the rotation drill.

5. You could activate three parts of the Shell Drill instead of just two parts. You should usually activate the parts of the Shell Drill that correspond to the offensive maneuvers of your next opponent.

XI. Defensive Stunts Using the Shell Drill:

A. Force Backdoor—Shoot the Gap

1. Player 1 can be compelled to hit 3 with a backdoor pass in two different ways. Diagram 10-28 shows X3 overplaying 3. Player 3 breaks backdoor; 1 passes to 3. In Diagram 10-29, 1 is being pressured by X1. Player 1 dribbles hard outside, and X3 races over to help X1 defend against the dribble (Closing the Gap). Player 3 breaks backdoor; 1 passes to 3.

2. In both cases, X4 comes over to stop the backdoor pass to 3. If X4 gets there in time, X4 steals the pass. If X4 gets there late (as the ball arrives to 3), X4 might be able to force a violation or draw the charge. If X4 gets to the reception a

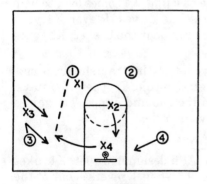

Diagram 10-28

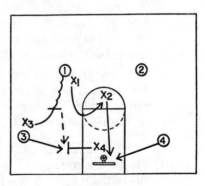

Diagram 10-29

little later, he merely calls the "rotation" drill (see Drill 55 or earlier section of the Shell Drill).

B. <u>Run-and-Jump Stunts:</u>

1. Player X1 forces 1 to drive at a considerable speed.

2. Player X3 (Diagram 10-30) or X2 (Diagram 10-31) calls a run and jump. The driver must be going toward a defender when a run and jump is called.

3. The defenders can be involved in a two-man run and jump (Diagram 10-31) or a three-man run and jump or a four-man run and jump (Diagram 10-30). You choose the number in the rotation.

4. Defenders can call "trap" or "used" instead of "jump" (see Drill 123).

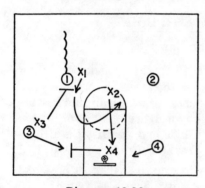

Diagram 10-30

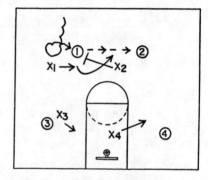

Diagram 10-31

C. <u>Trap Baseline Drives:</u>

1. Whenever 3 (or 4) drives the baseline, X4 comes over to help trap 3. This discourages baseline drives. Player X4 yells "trap." Player X2 zones the area near the basket; X1 zones the outside (Diagram 10-32).

2. You decide on the rotation out of the trap should a successful pass be made. Our rotation rule: Trapper (X4) stays; container (X3) rotates as in the run and jumps. That gives us a solid defense with only one rule.

D. <u>Give Outside—Take It Away</u>

1. Player X1 pressures 1 hard. At a designated spot, X1 takes the outside drive away from 1. When 1 reverses out of the defense of X1, X2 races over and traps. X4 guards 2 or 4 or splits them to shoot the gap (Diagram 10-33).

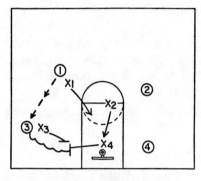

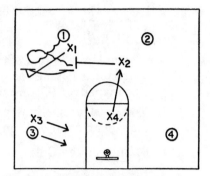

Diagram 10-32   Diagram 10-33

2. Player X2 can, if he arrives at the correct instant, force 1 to commit a turnover or can impel 1 to charge.

3. The rotation out of the trap is always the same: Trapper (X2) stays; container (X1) rotates.

4. Instead of trapping, X2 could have yelled "jump," activating the run and jumps.

E. The Peel Down:

1. Player X1 compels 1 to dribble quickly (Diagram 10-34).

2. Player X2 cheats toward the outside where 1 is driving hard; X2 comes over to stop 1's drive.

3. Player X1 yells "trap" or "jump," depending on what you want.

4. Player X3 denies 3 the ball; X4 plays, 2 or 4, or both.

5. Rotation is the same as in the other drills: Trapper (X2) stays; container (X1) rotates.

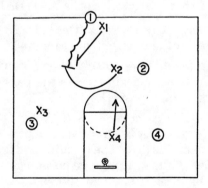

Diagram 10-34

XII. Some Odd Uses of the Shell:

A. Rub-Off:

1. Player 1 passes to 3 who uses 4 to rub his man off. Teams that run a double- or single-stack offense frequently use this maneuver (Diagram 10-35).

2. You must decide how you intend to defense this offensive maneuver, then drill on it.

B. The Shuffle Cut:

1. Player 1 passes to 4; X4 should have denied the flash pivot. Meanwhile, 3 has set a shuffle screen on X2 (Diagram 10-36).

2. Again you must decide the coverage you want on shuffle cuts. Your coverage should be consistent throughout your entire defensive system.

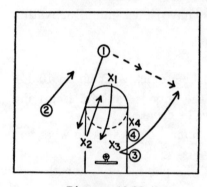   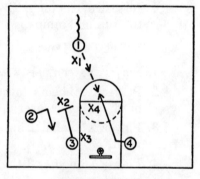

Diagram 10-35   Diagram 10-36

C. Some Other Ways to Use the Shell Drill:

1. *To relieve overplay.* Player 2 tries to free 3 for a penetrating pass to begin the offense (Diagram 10-37).

2. *To defend inside screen away.* Player 3 screens for 4; 4 goes out as far as he must to receive the pass from 2. Player 3 rolls back to high post (Diagram 10-38).

3. *To combine these maneuvers with the UCLA Power Cut.* Player 2 screens for 3; 3 receives the pass and 2 screens for 4. Player 4 moves along the baseline and 2 rolls back to high post. When 3 hits 4, 1 uses the power cut, making use of 2's screen (Diagrams 10-39 and 10-40).

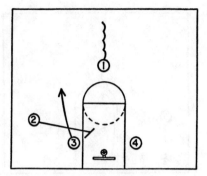

Diagram 10-37

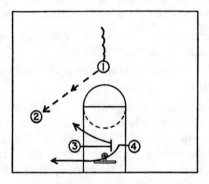

Diagram 10-38

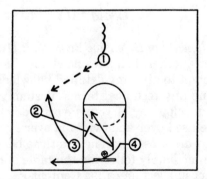

Diagram 10-39

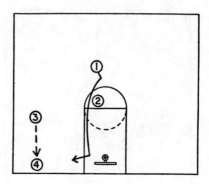

Diagram 10-40

4. As coach you must decide how to cover all of these maneuvers if your defense is to be ultrasuccessful.

5. You can use the Shell Game whether you plan to teach a man-to-man or a zone defense.

6. You can use only one maneuver or combine several or all of them while using the Shell Game.

7. You should, at the beginning of the year, divide your squad into teams of four. These teams can compete all winter long. You can keep records. At the end of the season, your teams will be very adept at playing the Shell Game, and at playing your team defense. While playing these Shell Games nightly, you should allow only the combination of cuts that your next opponent will use. Only occasionally should you permit "anything goes." After all, it is a learning situation.

SUMMARY

The *Encyclopedia of Defensive Basketball Drills* does not favor one defense over another. It makes no claim of teaching a defense. There is no attempt to give any detailed knowledge of any defense; nor does it define any technical terms. It simply offers drills that you can use to develop any of your favorite defenses. It is a reference work, to be used over and over and over again.

These drills are cross-referenced for the benefit of the reader. On the pages immediately following the table of contents, defenses are listed in a special section called Content Pages of Drills. Drills are numbered in this *Encyclopedia*. Those numbers are listed under the defenses in this special Content Pages of Drills section. Also, each drill as it is presented, has a number, a name, and a parenthesis with numbers inside the parenthesis. For example, Drill 1: Trio Drill (2, 3, 4, 7, 9). The numbers inside the parenthesis refer to the defenses that can make use of this drill. As a third cross-reference, the major teaching drills relating to any defense is included in the chapter on that defense. For example, Chapter 3 is devoted primarily to man defenses.

Besides the obvious advantages of the triple-tier cross-referencing, *Encyclopedia* offers four other major usages:

1. You can use it for practice planning.

2. As your season progresses, you can pick out drills that will correct specific training problems.

3. You have a virtual plethora of drills teaching the same point, ranging from single- to multipurpose, that you can switch in and out of practices to eliminate late season staleness.

4. Best of all, careful study of the book, especially Chapter 1, will show you, the coach, how you can design and use your own drills.

Index

206

T